Drift

"You're going to love this book! In it, Tim addresses how we can go from "drifting" through life to discovering and realizing our destiny. It's a book about hope, freedom and a new beginning. It's about breaking the power of your past and possessing the purpose, the true fulfillment for which you were created. He reminds us we have significance, that we are indeed God's Masterpiece and that it's never too late to "stop drifting."

— Pastor Zane Anderson, Zane Anderson Ministries

"Drift is a prophetic word delivered with grace. After identifying some key areas where we drift, Twigg leads us on a path to recovery. He does careful research as illustrated in Chapter 3 where he identifies loneliness as a major threat to young adults. His autobiographical pieces at the beginning and end are a nice touch. This book is more than a quick read and move on. It requires reflection and response. A timely word that should bear good fruit."

- H. Robert Rhoden, Author, Four Faces of a Leader

"*Drift*, by Tim Twigg, is a must read for any believer who has found themselves "drifting", whether that drift is spiritual, emotional, or otherwise. Tim's concise and often humorous look at the many ways we might find ourselves drifting and his insightful biblical remedies for these drifts are both well thought out and extraordinarily on point. As a writer, minister, and counselor, I see this kind of drift often. How wonderful to have a resource to share and quite frankly, to use for myself. Bravo, Tim!"

- Dr. Deb Waterbury, CEO of Deb Waterbury, LLC and Love Everlasting Ministries.

Drift

Finding Your Way Back When Life Throws You Off Course

Tim Twigg

ARROW
PRESS

Hardcover: 978-1-951475-07-9
Paperback: 978-1-951475-06-2
Ebook: 978-1-951475-08-6

Library of Congress Control Number: 2020937893

Edited by Avodah Editorial Services

Arrow Press Publishing
Summerville, SC
www.arrowpresspublishing.com

CONTENTS

FOREWORD

I first met Tim Twigg in 2005 when he came to work in the Youth Department of the Potomac District of the Assemblies of God. He is a GenXer. I am from the builder generation or what some call the silent generation. While more than thirty years separate us in age we connected in conversation and he adopted me as a spiritual father. Even after I retired and moved a hundred miles away we still maintained our connection.

Tim is a gifted wordsmith. DRIFT is a product of His keen mind and spiritual passion. But it's more than that. It is a prophetic word delivered with grace. He does careful research in identifying loneliness as a major threat to young adults. The five tripping points to watch for in success should be in everyone's notebook.

I wish I had thought of defining success as obedience to God. It is profound and brilliant. After identifying some key areas where we drift, Tim leads us on a path to recovery.

In a seamless manner he introduces one of my favorite quotes. "We judge ourselves by our intentions and others by their behavior," a Steven Covey line that helps us deal with blind spots. His autobiographical pieces at the beginning and end are a nice touch. DRIFT is not just an idea in Tim's mind. He lives what he writes.

I am captured by the idea of two unnamed songs that Tim engages with when he needs to visit his altars of remembrance. When you get to this place in the book I'm sure you will want to make your own altar of remembrance. It will be a moment to pay more careful attention to what we have read, so that we do not drift away (Hebrews 2:1).

This book is not merely a quick read and move on. It requires reflection and response. A timely word that I believe will bear good fruit!

Bob Rhoden
Author | The Four Faces of a Leader & Restless to Reconciled
Glen Allen, VA

I dedicate this book to my Family

To my father, thank you for always leading the way. You modeled what it looked like to stay committed to Jesus through good times and bad. Thank you for being a prayer warrior, teacher, and a great listener.
You are my hero.

To mom, thank you for sacrificing so much for us to succeed. You love your family without reserve and support without hesitation. Thank you for working so tirelessly to create a home of love, care, and security.

To my wife, you put up with the late nights of work, my dysfunctional drive to accomplish more, and my brain that never turns off. Yet, you keep me balanced, you are unflinchingly honest, and you're an incredible mom and wife. I literally could not have done this without you and your support. I love you.
We make a great team.

To my brother, thanks for always encouraging and believing in me. We made our share of mistakes growing up, but God has never left our side. Thanks for never leaving mine.

Finally, I dedicate this book to my daughter, Abygail. I've become a better follower of Jesus because of you. You have helped me understand Father God's love because of how much I love you. You're my favorite.

INTRODUCTION

YOU ARE NOT DRIFTWOOD

"A life that hasn't a definite plan is likely to become driftwood. - David Sarnoff"

"Can I ask you a question?" the man sitting next to me whispered.

Oh no, I thought. A question like that seems to never end well when you're confined in a plane, thirty-thousand feet above the ground. Many people love to talk to strangers on airplanes, but I'm not one of them. I had selected a window seat and was perfectly content staring aimlessly at the clouds. He must have seen the Bible on my lap and thought maybe I could help

"Sure," I replied. "What's up?"

I expected his question would be antagonistic toward my faith. Would he insist I believed in a myth? Would he ask whom I voted for? Would he present a well-structured debate on the problem of evil when believing in an infinitely good God?

It was none of the above. Instead, he spoke softly, "Can you say a prayer for me?"

My guard dropped. "Of course." I was more than relieved I wouldn't have to sit next to a religious combatant for the next three hours.

He swallowed. "My wife is leaving me, and I don't know what to do."

I wasn't sure how to respond. What combination of words can calm someone who is so desperately searching for answers? There are moments when God divinely and graciously inspires us to speak the right words at the right time. This was not that moment. I sat stunned and speechless. Even as I write this book, I can't fathom how desperate he must have been to share such pain with a stranger.

"I'm so sorry," I said. "Of course, I'll pray for you. If you don't mind me asking, what happened?"

More details would help me determine how to specifically intercede for his situation, but he wasn't prepared to share. I think he expected the conversation to end with my initial response, but he had taken a bold, uncomfortable step to share his hurt with a random passenger on a plane and I didn't want to offer a trite cookie-cutter prayer like, "Bless him, Lord. Give him wisdom and peace." I truly wanted those things for him, but I didn't want to just pray *for* him; I wanted to intercede *with* him.

He blinked repeatedly as his eyes shifted back and forth, fighting back tears. "I don't know. There were no signs. I thought everything was great. I honestly didn't see it coming. Then one day I came home from work and she hit me with the news. She was leaving me for a guy she met on the internet. I thought everything was great, but..." His voice trailed off. I could tell he was searching through every word spoken, every slighted look, for *any* sign he may have missed that his wife was about to leave him.

I listened to his story, we prayed together, and I encouraged him as best I could.

"Thank you," he said, and as if the conversation never happened, he closed his eyes and laid his head back against the uncomfortably small seat.

I waited for him to re-engage the conversation, but he never did. I, on the other hand, couldn't focus the rest of the flight. Question after question assaulted my mind. *How did he not see this coming? Is there something I'm missing in my marriage? No, my wife would never leave me. Wait, I'll bet there was a time he said that too. Am I a good husband? What would I do if she left?*

Have you ever been caught in an irrational thought loop? It typically doesn't end with joy. Have you ever had an innocent thought, only to see it dovetail into a bad memory or an inappropriate daydream? Our thought life is not cleanly compartmentalized. It is intertwined with poor decisions, triumphant victories, hurts, and heartaches. Taking these thoughts captive and submitting them to Christ is easier said than done. A thought adrift can be destructive, divisive, and depressing.

In the movie *Inception*, Leonardo DiCaprio's character, Cobb, makes a profound statement: "An idea is like a virus. Resilient. Highly contagious. And even the smallest seed of an idea can grow. It can grow to define or destroy you." The first time I heard it I immediately thought about the apostle Paul's exhortation to hold captive every thought that sets itself against the knowledge, revelation, and relational nature of God (2 Corinthians 10:5). If left unchecked, our thought life will always lead, never follow. In submitting our thoughts to Christ, we change the order of influence. The believer who can lead his thoughts can achieve the impossible.

I can usually shift mental gears quickly and move on, but not with the man on the airplane. I struggled to hold my thoughts captive. They were pressing against the cell doors in my mind, and no matter how hard I tried, I couldn't hold them back. The more I resisted, the more I failed. I thought about that man and his situation for weeks. His statement played over and over in my head: "There were no signs. I didn't see it coming. There were no signs. I didn't see it coming. There were no signs. I didn't see it coming." He wasn't lying. He truly didn't see it coming, but that doesn't mean the signs weren't there.

He didn't share a lot of details about his marriage and I'm sure if he had, I'd have received only one side of the story. Men can sometimes be out of touch with their emotional side, but to not see anything? There were *no* signs? After years of marriage there was *no* indication things had changed? Or was it that he refused to acknowledge changes he'd seen, for fear of the story they were telling?

How did he find himself in this place of shock and disbelief, unable to make sense of what was happening around him? Could all of this have been avoided? I never saw this man again, but the evidence pointed to a universal problem we've all experienced. He drifted.

Everyone suffers from *the drift* at some point in their life. Unfortunately, we never drift toward a better version of ourselves. We don't accidentally get in shape, become wealthy, have a great marriage, get promoted, or grow spiritually. Instead, we embody the very essence of the word *drift*. We wander aimlessly, carried about with little to no resistance. No one drifts to a destination they desire. People only drift to detrimental places.

Drifting is deceptive in that it confuses movement with advancement. If you've ever enjoyed fishing or camping near a river or lake, you've likely come in contact with driftwood. High winds, storms, or logging can cause a tree limb to fall into a river, and it eventually finds its way to a riverbank or the ocean shore. The wood has been severed from its life source and is quite dead, but for a time it is still moving. It thrashes back and forth in the river rapids or floats on an ocean current. Dead, but still moving.

Perhaps this is how you feel right now. Dead, but still moving.

Jesus has a lot to say about driftwood. Well, maybe not about driftwood specifically, but it plays. In John 15:5–7, He exhorts, "I am the vine; you are the branches. Whoever abides in me and I in him, it is he that bears much fruit, for apart from me you can do nothing. If anyone does not abide in me he is thrown away like a branch and withers; and the branches are gathered, thrown into the fire, and burned. If you abide in me, and my words abide in you, ask whatever you wish, and it will be done for you" (ESV).

That sounds like driftwood to me. When connected to the vine, the branch fulfills its purpose and produces fruit. The Bible doesn't specify what kind of fruit. Fruit can look quite different to different people. One person's fruit may take the form of caring for the homeless. Another person's fruit is seen in the emotional healing of a trafficked young girl. We get into trouble when we judge the validity of someone else's fruit based on the shape and size of our own.

The branch stops producing when it is separated from the vine. When we are detached from the nourishment and instruction of Holy Spirit, we find ourselves drifting. Have you ever wondered why some sway with the waves of culture, letting the tide of the times dictate their course? They're disconnected from the vine. They have become driftwood. It is in this context that we find two paths, both of which are ours to choose. If we stay connected to the vine, we can ask whatever we wish and it will be done for us. Detach from the vine and we'll be gathered and thrown into the fire. The choice is yours, although it should be no choice at all.

Driftwood burns extremely well when it has had the opportunity to dry out. That's **not** a good thing if **you** are the driftwood. The goal of the tree branch is not to spread its leaves and fly. There is no innate desire for foliage independence. The tree limb also never purposes to end up a decaying piece of land art. It was created to flourish, grow, provide oxygen and fruit, and contribute to the global ecosystem—but only if it is connected to the source.

If movement were the indicator of intention, driftwood would be quite influential. In reality, it is simply a tree limb robbed of its purpose, destined to wash up. This piece of wood was once connected, abundant, and life giving, but is now nothing more than an obstruction; a decaying piece of timber.

We never expect to drift. The cause of the drift is different for everyone. Perhaps it was a personal tragedy, a relational wound, besetting sin, or even success that caused you to drift. Regrettably, it's not until you wash up on the shore that you realize the person you are isn't the one you intended to become. Pain has the uncanny knack of instilling intense moments of clarity.

We don't drift on purpose. It's not that we choose to lay dormant until the negative overtakes us and we find ourselves in an emotional pit. The drift is subtle. If it were drastic, I believe we would act sooner and with a greater sense of urgency.

We see this example in aviation. If you were to take a flight from Washington, D.C. to Los Angeles, you would fly approximately 2,300 miles. If your flight is just one degree off course, it would deviate 92 feet for every mile. This means by the time you arrive in California, you would be approximately 40 miles off course. If you leave D.C. and attempt to travel around the world, just one degree off and you will not land back in Washington D.C. You would land in Boston, Massachusetts, over 400 miles away. It's the drift. It is destructive because of its subtlety.

Maybe this is why the man on the plane didn't see it coming. Maybe the signs were there, but they seemed so minuscule he never thought they'd make a difference. He was drifting and just didn't know it.

Maybe you are drifting now. You feel dead inside but you're still moving.

Driftwood cannot be brought back to life, but you are not driftwood, even if you temporarily take on its characteristics. You are God's masterpiece, His craftsmanship, His beloved. Outside of violating His own character, there is no distance He will not traverse to reach you, restore you, and bring wholeness to your situation.

That is the purpose of this book. This book is for the imperfect. It's for the person who didn't see the signs, only the fallout. It's for the person who wants to guard against the drift. It's for the person who refuses to let life happen to them with no recourse.

My desire for this book is two-fold. First, it is a prevention tool. Perhaps you'll see yourself in one of the eight drift catalysts, and it will be enough to establish proper boundaries in safe places. Second, it is to inspire immediate course correction. You may be living in the aftermath of a life that drifted, but that doesn't mean you need to stay there. You can find your bearings again. God's desire is to restore you, not leave you stranded. Jesus is tossing you a lifeline, and He needs you to grab on. He has too much purpose for you to simply leave you adrift.

In this book I've outlined eight significant drift catalysts. Most of us have experienced one or more of these drift starters. While you may be tempted to jump straight to the chapter that would most impact your current situation, my recommendation is to read it straight through. We are often drifting in several directions, and they are often linked together. Processing through this book from start to finish will ensure nothing remains hidden.

Remember, even though you may be drifting, you are not alone. I've drifted more times than I can count. Those drifts have led to some indescribably painful experiences, but I have seen God's faithfulness and I know He works all things for the good (Romans 8:28). I pray that what I've learned along the way can help you stay the course when life happens to you—that you'll become the rudder and not the sail.

Years later, I still think about the man on the plane. I wonder where he landed.

PART ONE

UNDERSTANDING THE DRIFT

"I understood myself only after I destroyed myself. And only in the process of fixing myself, did I know who I really was."

— Sade Andria Zabala

ONE

. . . .

THE PAIN DRIFT

Many people, when describing negative experiences, use a popular phrase: "life happens." They're not referring to the good stuff. They're referring to the bad stuff that seems to occur more often than we'd like. And when "life happens" to us, we find ourselves surprised, offended, and confused. We ask why, as if knowing the reason would somehow make the trial easier. It would only lead to more questions and more insistence that we don't deserve what we are getting.

I regularly reflect on a statement by journalist and author Sydney Harris. He noted, "Whenever I hear someone sigh, 'Life is hard,' I am always tempted to ask, 'Compared to what?'"

Life can be unrelenting. You can't play a magical combination of numbers and hit the life lotto. There is only life. The decisions we make in life determine our capacity and resolve when "life happens." Suffering never feels fair, but fair is a misguided illusion. One person's fair is another person's offense. Jesus was perfect and even He had to weather betrayal, doubt, torture, hate, and loneliness. Nothing was fair about Jesus giving Himself for my sins, yet there He was, in pain, for me.

Being born with advantages doesn't reduce the reality that every individual will one day need to take ownership of the life they've been given. History is littered with stories of the millionaires who lose everything and the urban poor who become brain surgeons. Every story is different, and every struggle has a measure of perspective in tow, but in the end the quality of your life will be the sum total of the choices you make and who you allow to lead it. While your choices may affect your identity, they don't define you.

My friend, Dr. Deb Waterbury, provides some insight in her book, *The Lies that Bind: And the Truth that Sets You Free*. She writes:

> *We are fallen, yes. We are sinful, yes. We don't deserve all that our Savior accomplished on our behalf, yes. We are nothing without Jesus, yes. But those things don't define us. These are realities and truths, but who we are is identified by our relationship with Christ, the One whose propitiation resulted in our receiving His righteousness by imputation. My identity, your identity, is Jesus.*

Yet, we filter everything through our pain-stained choices and not through Jesus' sacrifice of love. We either understand the pain in the light of **our** poor choices, or we understand pain in the

17

light of the poor choices of **others**. It's easier to process pain when it has a clear cause.

I have a friend who, in anger, punched a wall. Instead of penetrating the drywall, he hit a stud and broke several bones in his hand. It wasn't the stud's fault. My friend had only himself to blame for mishandling his frustration. The cause and effect was quite clear, there was no confusing the source of his pain. Misaligned anger + irrational behavior = broken bones. His pain had a clear cause.

But what about the pain that comes from choices you don't make? What about the pain that comes through the actions of others? My brother worked at a railroad for nearly thirteen years before being laid off. He wasn't laid off because he was bad at his job. He wasn't unfaithful, inconsistent, or a lazy worker. On the contrary, he showed up early, worked overtime regularly, and did what he was asked with excellence, and yet he was still the unfortunate casualty of a company that chose to restructure and downsize. It wasn't his fault, but the pain and struggle fell on him just the same, and he was forced to move, sell his house, and find a new job in a different state.

For you it may have been a family member, a company, or a boss who made your life miserable. Maybe it was your own moment of poor judgment that caused your pain. Those scenarios are clean. There is a villain, even if the villain is our own insensibility.

Then there are the most perplexing of scenarios. What do you do when the pain isn't because of your mistake **or** the choice of another?

ABYGAIL

My wife and I weren't so lucky when we had our first child. On March 29, 2017, my wife was five months pregnant. I had just finished preaching at our Wednesday night church service when Mitch, a friend of over twenty years approached and handed me a note. "God gave me a word for you while you were speaking. I wrote it down," he said as he handed me some scribbles on a piece of paper. It read:

I have and am doing an incredible powerful work in and through you. I will do things through you that will change lives and this world. A testing is coming that I have equipped you for. Do not look to the left or the right. Keep your eyes on me and watch... It's going to be awesome.

I liked the first part. The second part made me feel rather uneasy. It was ominous and vague and provided no timeline for this testing. I knew my friend was not spiritually flippant. God had given him the spiritual gifts of discernment and prophecy, so I leaned in. Being planted in a healthy prophetic environment, I've learned even if a prophetic word does not apply in the moment, it may be valid for a future season. I took a picture of the note and kept it for later reference. I had no idea the time of testing would come in just a few months, and I had no idea the test would include nearly losing my wife and child.

My wife was scheduled to be induced on July 30, 2017. She was already one week past her due date. We woke up feeling prepared and joyful, unaware this would be the worst week of our lives.

We prayed for a smooth labor experience, but quickly realized this was not to be our story. My wife was in labor for thirty-six hours.

The time finally came for us to meet Abygail, but after only a few minutes of pushing, the doctor realized something was wrong. She looked at us and said, "We need to do an emergency cesarean—now. There is meconium in your baby's lungs."

We didn't know it at the time, but meconium aspiration syndrome is a leading cause of severe illness and death in a newborn. Yet, even though this had been a strenuous experience, we were more excited than fearful. We knew that in just a few minutes our daughter, our first child, would be in our arms.

We were wrong.

As I sat outside the operating room, the neonatologist approached and sat down beside me. Not knowing the severity of the situation, I didn't fully process what he said until much later. "We're going to do everything we can for your wife and baby. We're going to have to work quick." It didn't compute. I was just excited to see my baby girl.

At 9:19 p.m. on July 31, Abygail Victoria Twigg was born. I barely caught a glimpse of her before the neonatologist and his team tugged her away. They didn't look in our direction or explain what they were doing; there was no time. They worked feverishly and focused solely on my baby, doing whatever they could to make sure she survived.

I didn't hear the baby's first cry, I didn't get to cut the umbilical cord, and my wife didn't get to hold her little girl. This was not the joyful experience you see on television or hear about from friends. This was a nightmare and it was impossible to wake up.

After the cesarean, I followed my daughter and the team to the NICU. I had never met this particular doctor prior to that day, yet somehow, he knew I was a pastor. With his Russian accent, he exhorted, "You are preacher. I believe in God. I do. Our connection, not so good, but I believe in Him. The best I can say is, this baby is in God's hands now."

He presented me with the option of taking my baby to the University of Arizona Banner Medical Facility for an experimental treatment to help with her acidosis. I didn't know what to do. How could I make this decision in such an overwhelmed mental state? What if I made the wrong decision and things got worse? I was exhausted, confused, and had never felt so helpless.

While he was explaining to me the harsh reality that my daughter might never be a typical child, might suffer from brain trauma, or worse, might not survive the night, a nurse ran into the NICU. She stared at me, slightly out of breath, and said, "Dad, come quickly. Your wife is hemorrhaging."

With no time to think, I ran down the hallway to the room where I thought my wife was recovering comfortably. As I walked into the room, a nurse told my wife, "We've got to do an emergency hysterectomy. You are bleeding out. We have to try to save your life." The female doctor offered me the opportunity to pray with my wife before they rushed her off.

The human body carries nearly six liters of blood. By the end of this trauma, my wife had lost four. They had to get the bleeding to stop or she would die. I signed a consent form and seconds later I was left sitting in our room, alone, faced with the very real possibility that I might lose both my wife and my daughter. What was supposed to be one of the happiest days of my life turned into the worst day of my life in only thirty minutes.

Thoughts flooded my mind. Thoughts no man should ever need to think. The thought of going home without my wife. The pictures, the stuff, the memories all linked to her. Then another realization hit. I would never have a son. I'd always wanted a son. I dreamed of having a son.

I broke. It was too much for my tired mind to process. I wept. What else could I do? After a few minutes, I stood up, looked in the mirror, and made a conscious decision to not waste my mental and emotional energy blaming God or asking Him for an explanation. After all, what good would knowing *why* do? Would it change the situation? Would it make the circumstance easier? No. Besides, even if an explanation was offered, I doubt I would have accepted it.

Because I have a relationship with Father God, I know that He is for me, not against me (Romans 8:31). I know He binds the brokenhearted (Psalm 147:3). I know He is near to those that call on Him (Psalm 145:18). I know that He hears my cries, sees my tears, and is concerned for my suffering (Exodus 3:7). I know He is my Comforter (2 Corinthians 1:3–5). All I could do was lean into His presence and hope to find some measure of solace there.

I refused to blame Him. I know He did not cause my suffering, so I had to trust that He would bring me through it. How could I dare reject the Comforter in the moment I needed Him the most? As a pastor, I am frequently confronted with people who are experiencing great pain and tragedy. I always encourage them to worship through the pain. It sounds counterintuitive, because it is. Our default is to curse, question, and condemn. Worship, however, becomes an invitation to our heavenly Father, asking Him to heal the wounded places, restore right perspective, and impart grace in the weariness.

Now I had to take my own advice. I played "Even When It Hurts" by Hillsong repeatedly. As I worshiped, I prayed. Prayer, in this instance, would be my greatest resource. I declared healing, protection, mercy, and faith. I began to bind on earth, believing it would be bound in heaven, and I chose to exercise my God-given authority. I prayed for the doctors, that God would give them wisdom and steady their hands. I prayed His will as best I could, and when I couldn't muster any more words, I prayed in the Spirit.

My father went to the church to pray, my mother was praying in the hospital lobby, and my brother was praying in Maryland. My friend Scott and his wife, Sarah, came to the hospital to encourage me and pray as well. My pastor and his wife were in a different state, but they immediately interceded for my wife and daughter when they heard the news. My spiritual father was praying for me in Virginia, and of course my closest spiritual brothers and sisters were interceding from, quite literally, all over the world.

I pulled myself together and began to gather our personal items. Suddenly it hit me. The note. Mitch's note. I scrolled through my phone until I found the picture and I read it again.

Do not look to the left or the right. Keep your eyes on me.

The doctor was in the NICU, waiting on an answer. Should I fly my daughter to the University of Arizona for experimental medical treatment? I summoned what little faith I had in the moment, walked back to the NICU, and prayed over my daughter. I looked at the doctor and said, "I'm keeping my daughter here. People are praying in the lobby, and an environment of prayer is the best place for her. I'm not transporting my daughter to the University of Arizona."

I knew in my heart that God could heal her just as easily where we were. I didn't need to do a thing. Just trust and pray. When I walked outside to get some air, I saw Dave, a man who served on the prayer team at our church. He was walking around the hospital, praying for my daughter. That memory still blesses me more than he'll ever know. I felt covered in prayer like never before.

I can't tell you how hard it was to put my faith in God in that moment. The idea that a wrong decision could cost my daughter her life took my breath away. After only a few minutes, the doctor returned with a lab report. Much to his surprise, and with a partially baffled facial expression, he said, "Your daughter's acidity levels have already begun to drop. Keep praying."

By midnight the acidosis was completely gone.

I wish I could say I expected God to heal my daughter quickly, but I didn't. I can't say I had the faith in that moment to expect much of anything. I received word that my wife came through the surgery and was transported to the CVICU. My daughter was in the NICU. I was sitting alone, at two thirty in the morning, clinging to a prophetic note, unsure of what would happen next. I just knew they were alive, and that knowledge gave me enough comfort to lay my head down and rest.

By the end of the next day, things began to turn around and my wife was transported out of the CVICU back to the Women's Birthing Center. The nurses and staff literally applauded and gave us hugs when we arrived. A couple of days later, my wife was finally able to see her daughter and hold her for the first time. It was one of the most emotionally raw moments I'd ever experienced. The nurses kept calling Abygail our miracle baby.

On Sunday, August 6, as we prepared to be discharged from the hospital, my wife and I took communion together. We opened a plastic container of hospital apple juice, grabbed a pack of crackers, prayed, and worshiped together. We were thankful, and we chose to remember God's goodness. We chose to remember His grace. We chose to seek His presence, not run from it. We chose joy, and we built an altar of remembrance; it was the time He turned a nightmare into a healthy, spirited newborn baby. One week earlier I had been told my daughter and wife might not survive, but on August 6 we were walking out of the hospital, victorious. The meconium was cleared from my daughter's lungs, her acidosis was gone, and all her organs were functioning as they should.

A few days later, we visited our pediatrician. He was astonished at our healthy little girl. He said in amazement, "If I hadn't seen her hospital summary and if I didn't know all that she had been through, I would have thought this was a healthy, natural birth." I mentioned my wife was also in ICU during that time. He lingered for another fifteen minutes, grilling us about our experience. In disbelief he stated, "Knowing what you've been through, I've never seen such a calm couple."

"Prayer works," I responded.

In times of desperation, you need people around you who are willing to storm the enemy gates and fight with unprecedented boldness. You don't need timidity and poise in those moments. You want ferocious prayers and relentless prayer warriors. I firmly believe my wife and daughter would not be with me today if not for a praying church, praying family, and praying friends. What the Enemy sought for harm, God turned into a miracle.

THE AFTERMATH

What I didn't expect from my pain was the aftermath. Maybe it was the physical exhaustion of sleeping on a hospital sofa every night for a week, or the sleep deprivation of a newborn baby, but I drifted. The pain of the experience took over and the things that needed my attention were neglected. That might be okay for a season, even necessary considering what we went through, but nobody ever warned me about the pain drift.

Pain pushes us into a survival mentality. Problems begin to arise when the initial pain subsides. People often have trouble re-engaging with responsibilities that were shirked during the storm. I thought things would return to "normal." They didn't. I struggled to re-engage with the same intensity I had before. It affected my relationships, my work, and my confidence.

I didn't know it then, but the mental fog I experienced is not uncommon. It is often seen when people endure a traumatic experience. When war veterans attempt to assimilate back into society, some struggle to hold a job. They live in a perpetual state of anxiety and fear, and some need to relearn to do the basic tasks many of us take for granted, like writing a resume or choosing what toilet paper to buy. The Pew Research Center noted that veterans who experienced a traumatic event or were seriously injured had the hardest time re-entering civilian life, versus those who served without wartime experience. Flashbacks and post-traumatic stress greatly reduce their ability to acclimate. I could never compare what I went through with someone who survived the trauma of war and loss, but I can relate to the lingering effects of pain, even after the trauma passes.

Months passed before I felt connected to my daughter. I felt like a fraud and a terrible father. I had heard the stories about the "instant love" that occurs when one sees their child for the first time. I never felt that love. The residue of pain caused me to drift to an unhealthy place, and I had to battle to love my daughter like a father should. It wasn't her fault. It wasn't my wife's fault. It wasn't my fault. It wasn't God's fault. It was life, it was painful, and it took time to walk in joy again. If I'm honest, a part of me is still clawing back.

Whenever I wonder if God has forgotten me in my drifting, I reflect on a verse from one of David's psalms: "You have kept count of my tossings; put my tears in your bottle. Are they not in your book?" (Psalm 56:8 ESV).

The word *tossing* can also be translated "wandering, to be aimless, to drift." There has never been a time you drifted that God didn't notice and chart your course home. He has made note of every time you've drifted and recorded every resulting pain, not to justify your punishment but to plot your redemption. Even when I thought I was drifting, God was tracking.

From your conception, God has seen every tear, every anxious moment, and every faithless decision. He sees all, knows all, and still passionately loves you. He knows *all* of you, and it hasn't changed His mind about you one bit. He still devotedly pursues you and yearns for a relationship with you. He is crazy about you.

Whether you realize it or not, a time will come when who you've been historically becomes history impacted by His story. A time will come when how you feel now will be a memory of the past and no longer a present reality.

Hold on. Don't you dare give up.

CAPTURING THE MOMENTS

When the cell phone began replacing the camera and video recorder, our lives became documented like never before. My parents have two or three photo albums of my life. They have dozens of pictures from birthdays, holidays, and other special events. I currently have hundreds of pictures *and* videos of my daughter and she's only two years old. When she grows up, she will have the best and worst moments of her life captured in the palm of her hand. Decades of ups and downs, bad hair days, and great dates. Well, maybe not dates. She can date when she's eighty-nine.

God has recorded *every* moment of your life, and He has stored up all your tears. In other words, your pain is not wasted. No one is immune from painful ordeals of life. Pain will alter your course and that new course may not be the one God intends for you. Pain has the power to forcefully transform our identity. It can petrify a soft heart. It can mutate a loving person into a distant, disconnected, and isolated hermit. A trusting person can become cynical, a happy person can become sorrowful, and a giving person can become greedy.

Everybody responds differently to pain. For some, pain punishes. For others, pain purifies. But for every piercing, there is a promise of proximity. God's encouragement to Joshua in Deuteronomy 31:6 still rings true today: "Be strong and courageous. Do not be afraid or terrified because of them, for the Lord your God goes with you; he will never leave you or forsake you."

If I'm honest, sometimes I'd prefer painless isolation to painful proximity; however, it's the very proximity we flee from that brings us peace. God is our Comforter because He knows we'll experience discomfort. It's who He has to be so that we can become who we were ordained to be.

Jesus was not impervious to life's woundings. Even He needed to be comforted. When Jesus was in the garden of Gethsemane, the very thought of what He was about to experience caused him to sweat drops of blood. The medical condition is called hematohidrosis. It occurs under conditions of extreme physical or emotional stress. Blood vessels in the skin break open and blood finds its way into the sweat glands.

Jesus knew how the events would unfold over the next few days of His life, and while fully God, He was also fully human, and his flesh recoiled at the thought of the impending torture. He asked the Father if there was an alternative plan, one that would permit Him to avoid the pain. He asked if the cup of suffering could be taken from Him.

The answer was no.

In the Old Testament, the "cup" is often used as a metaphor of an individual's fate or condition. That cup can be positive or negative (Psalm 23:5; 116:13; Isaiah 51:17; Ezekiel 23:33; Isaiah 51:17). In this moment, not only did Jesus profess His understanding of the pain He must endure for the redemption of humankind, He also confessed the frailty of His flesh. It's challenging enough when one experiences unexpected pain. It's an entirely different thing when one endures chosen pain.

Jesus did not allow His pain to cause Him to drift off course and, in His obedience to the Father, set before us a model to follow.

Pain does not have to close you off, steer you away, or push you into isolation. Pain does not have to be your purpose, and it does not have to be your legacy. We acknowledge Jesus' pain and suffering, but we celebrate His resurrection. Jesus made sure His pain was purposeful. Don't waste your pain on self-loathing, bitterness, or un-forgiveness.

Perhaps it's time for your resurrection. Your pain may have thrown you off course for weeks, months, or years, but I have good news. Jesus is an incredible cartographer. He knows exactly where you are on the map, and He knows the quickest route back to wholeness.

You may be thinking, *But, Tim, you don't know what I'm going through!*

I don't. What you are experiencing may make my personal tragedy look like a walk in the park on a sunny day. Even so, don't let the drift become your destiny. Your course correction may take time, often dependent upon how far you've drifted, but the decision to get back on course can be made today.

I want to give you a couple of things to meditate on as you process your pain:

I. Pain is Not Permanent

This is not intended to be a callous or dismissive statement. Your pain may literally result in the end of your life, yet my statement stands true. For most, your current pain level will decrease, and you'll find yourself in a season of prosperity again. Learn what you need to learn in the pain, and plan what you'll do when the season of suffering ends.

Many times, the length of our suffering is often our doing. If you have the ability to move on, move on. Don't linger longer than you need to. Pain may be temporary, but unfortunately, you have the power to make it permanent. I implore you to move on in due season. One day your pain *will* end, and if you have a relationship with Jesus Christ, you'll stand before Him completely healed and whole for all eternity. In the present or in things to come, pain has an expiration date.

II. Pain Should Not Be Wasted

Is there a lesson in the pain? Who are you now because of the pain? What are you now aware of?

High school can be a turbulent time, and no more so than for the student who fails a grade. Nobody likes being held back in school. It's frustrating, humiliating, and a waste of time. Of course, we doctor up the terminology. The student doesn't "fail"; they simply need to repeat the grade. Don't be that person. Don't repeat your pain unnecessarily. Take out your journal, make note of what you've learned and what you'll do different, and move on with your hard-learned lessons.

The apostle Paul boasted in his weakness so that Christ's power would rest on him and he'd be made perfect. Pain submitted will create greater intimacy with God the Father, and the day may come when you boast about God's restoration in your life.

III. Pain Should Not Be Private

Few may fully understand what you are going through, but that doesn't mean they are not called to help you carry your burden. We are commanded to encourage one another (1 Thessalonians

5:11), pray for one another (James 5:16), and bear one another's burdens (Galatians 6:2).

The Enemy wants to isolate you, mess with your mind, convince you nobody cares, and create a permanent divide between you and the body of Christ. The quicker you invite others into your hurt, the quicker you'll find healing. Find a group, call a friend, or get some lunch with a mentor or coach. Isolation may be necessary for a moment as you process your pain, but please don't stay there. When isolated and alone, you are exposed to the onslaught of the Enemy, who desires to steal your purpose through private pain.

IV. Pain is Puppy Love

Puppy love is a term used to describe an intense but shallow romantic attachment associated with adolescents. It's a quaint little phrase with one glaring oversight; puppy love is real to puppies. It may be shallow from the outside looking in, but it's quite real to the those in the midst of the attraction. Adults downplay the depth. "They don't know what real love is," we quip. Yet puppy love brings heartache, tears, severed relationships, and broken trust. The effects of puppy love should never be devalued. Suicides occur over puppy love.

There is the tendency to treat the pain of others like puppy love. If one opines that the depth of another's suffering is less than theirs, we will whitewash their pain and minimize its impact. We may be right, but for that individual, their pain may be the worst they've ever experienced. This isn't a competition, certainly not one you'd care to win. It is not our responsibility to judge who has suffered the most, who deserves their suffering, or who should be declared martyr of the year. Don't let your pain desensitize you to the pain of others. Empathy, like love, is not a limited commodity. You don't have to pick and choose who receives your empathy. Give it freely. You may find it returned to you in greater measure.

Get Through, Not Over

Finally, be patient. One of the most callous things a person can say to someone going through a painful experience is "You need to get over it." If you've ever suffered and been given that advice, you likely felt the immediate urge to learn Krav Maga and challenge them to a duel. You may be tempted to sarcastically respond, "You know what? You're right. I'm glad you've given me such amazing guidance. Done. I'm over it. Whew, that's better."

If "getting over it" were easy, it would have happened a long time ago. In his famous psalm, David declared, "Even though I walk through the darkest valley, I will fear no evil, for you are with me" (Psalm 23:4). David didn't go around the dark valley. He went *through* the dark valley. If you are currently in a painful place, or if you experienced pain a long time ago yet it still feels fresh today, don't let anyone tell you to simply "get over it." You will, however, need to "get through it." David didn't camp out in the dark valley; his promise was waiting on the other side.

Pain can cause you to drift from your relationships, your calling, your career, and even your purpose. It will convince you no one understands what you are going through. It will usher in confusion and exhausting toil. It will cycle you from valley to valley, never gracing you with the perspective of the mountaintop.

If you are stuck in a cycle of pain and it has changed you into a person you don't recognize, it's time. It's time to find yourself again and nobody knows you better than Jesus. Take a moment right now to confess your pain to your heavenly Father. You may cry, you may feel a heat wave of anger or frustration, or you may feel numb, but God will never waste your pain. I wish I could tell you your pain will vanish instantly. For some it will, but for others it will be a process. Your job isn't to heal yourself. Your job is to position yourself to receive the healing of the Father.

You may not have caused your pain, but God will use your pain and supernaturally reconstruct it into something beautiful. What people may have meant for evil, God may use to save a generation (Genesis 50:20).

At the time of this writing, my daughter is three years old and my love for her grows exponentially every day. She's daddy's little girl. Each morning on the way to daycare, we listen to worship music. She has her own playlist of kids worship songs. Every morning without fail she asserts in her sweet little voice, "Daddy, I want to listen to 'Jesus Loves Me.'"

If she only knew how much.

TWO

....

THE PAST DRIFT

My heart dropped in my chest and for a split second I couldn't breathe. My friend had just delivered some agonizing news. In a moment of soul neglect and poor judgment, he had been unfaithful to his wife.

This scenario may be a familiar one in today's culture that focuses on self-gratification above interpersonal health, but it does not make it any easier to navigate. I did my best to encourage him and prayed He would come to understand God's grace, mercy, and forgiveness. Just as he did not earn his salvation prior to this incident, he couldn't earn forgiveness after. It was simply a gift that he had to accept. That was the problem.

His wife had forgiven him, her family had forgiven him, and his friends had forgiven him. We reassured him we weren't going anywhere, but it wasn't enough. He was stuck in a destructive cycle of despair and self-deprecation. He not only refused to accept the reality of forgiveness, but also insisted on mentally punishing himself, which led to sleepless nights, stress, fatigue, and physical sickness.

We had many more conversations after that day, and through those conversations he began to search for answers to questions he didn't even know to ask. What emerged was a pattern that was not formed from his present circumstance. He realized he had been giving himself permission to live in a way that fed his flesh and starved his spirit. It finally caught up with him, and in a malnourished spiritual state, he stumbled and fell.

If you've ever been in this place, you can relate to the disgusting feeling my friend felt. It gnaws at your stomach and permeates your whole body. It's the feeling when you say goodbye to a loved one who passes away. It's the feeling of loss, confusion, and helplessness. It's the feeling of a sacrificed future.

Christians are often conflicted when they hear stories of infidelity. There are some who strive to build up and some who strive to break up. You'll inevitably hear well-meaning Christians condemn, convict, and sentence the malefactor to relational death with no trial or appeal.

I understand the depth of hurt and pain that comes from broken trust with someone you truly care for, and I struggle with the messy reality in which God loves the **villain** as much as He loves the **victim**. Yet I also realize, in my life, I've been both. I've been the betrayer of trust and I've been the victim of good faith broken badly. I've been the recipient of unjustified, as well as justified, condemnation. I've inflicted pain and suffering on others relationally and emotionally. I've been the one who shattered confidences, betrayed trust, and left people confused as to why I would "do such a thing." If we're honest, we've all been the villain a time or two (or three, or four, or one hundred).

Each of us has a story, and if we all told **our** story, our **real** story, we would realize we have been the one Jesus left the ninety-nine to find. Instead, we cast detailed judgment without accurate details, yet we do not have the right to look at **anyone** and call them "too far gone."

As a follower of Christ, your default must be the belief that Jesus can restore all things, but you also have to address the thing that has subversively caused you to drift. In many instances, it's your past.

DRIFTWOOD NEVER RETURNS

Driftwood never returns to its point of origin. Eventually driftwood's journey will end, and it will wash up on the shore. There are no scenarios in which driftwood magically returns to the moment when it was severed from its source. Only humanity thinks this way. **You** think this way.

You may be there right now. If you've ever made the statement "If only I could go back" or "I've been playing the moment over and over in my mind. If only I had _____, then things would be different," congratulations, you are now a part of a very inclusive club. This club is filled with billions of people who have made mistakes yet believe theirs is the worst of them all.

Don't worry, you don't have to stay in the club. In fact, you can turn in your membership card today. Going back in time is not the answer, and despite your love of sci-fi movies, it's not possible. Even though time travel is a concept of science fiction, as a culture we are attracted to the possibilities. I love watching time-travel movies. The ability to travel back in time to change your future and immediately see the impact in the present is a brilliant concept, but it's not real. Say it with me: It's. Not. Real. If I'm honest, I wish it were. There are so many things I would do differently. There are a lot of things you'd do differently, but those things are no longer in our control. We can only cast our gaze to the future and put our efforts into creating the future we envision by God's grace and guidance. It may be hard, but you'll have to get rid of the notion you can change the past.

I like to get rid of things. I'm a minimalist. If I don't use it or if it does not have significant sentimental meaning, I get rid of it. I despise clutter. I want everything I own to add value to my life, not just exist in my life. One year we moved across the country and had to pack up our house. We started emptying out our pantry and my wife commented, "If it's expired, throw it away."

I ended up throwing away half of the miscellaneous food in our pantry. It had accumulated over the months and years, and left unchecked, it began to take up a lot of space that could have been reserved for more useful items. Some items had expired four years prior! I remember opening the pantry and being so irritated because it was overly full to the point that things would fall off the shelves when I was looking for an item. If only I had taken assessment of what had outlived its shelf life but still took up space.

Your past has a shelf life. Your past was crucified with Christ on that fateful day. Paul echoes this sentiment in Galatians 2:20 when he declares, "I have been crucified with Christ and I no longer live, but Christ lives in me. The life I now live in the body, I live by faith in the Son of God, who loved me and gave himself for me."

If your life is no longer your life, then your past is no longer yours either. It's His, and He is not spending one moment thinking about it. Don't waste your life trying to redeem what He has already redeemed. Instead of reverting back to your marred history, do this one thing. Forget what is behind and strain toward what is ahead. Press on, don't quit, and don't look back. Straining for the prize is part of the process. Our past will always exist to remind us we don't deserve to be where we are, but our success comes when we give Christ permission to redeem our history, give purpose to our present, and mark the path for our future.

You may not be able to jump into a souped-up DeLorean and travel back in time to change your life, but that's the point. When we are in Christ; we don't have to. If any person be in Christ Jesus, they are a new creation. The old has gone, the new has come (2 Corinthians 5:17).

In his letter to the church at Philippi, Paul writes:

I want to know Christ—yes, to know the power of his resurrection and participation in his sufferings, becoming like him in his death, and so, somehow, attaining to the resurrection from the dead. Not that I have already obtained all this, or have already arrived at my goal, but I press on to take hold of that for which Christ Jesus took hold of me. Brothers and sisters, I do not consider myself yet to have taken hold of it. But one thing I do: Forgetting what is behind and straining toward what is ahead, I press on toward the goal to win the prize for which God has called me heavenward in Christ Je-sus. (Philippians 3:10–15)

Before Paul could fully and completely press on, he had to become forgetful. He had to embrace what he had overcome and choose to not look on those things that lingered in the back of his mind. We sabotage ourselves when we let the mistakes that belong in our past affect our judgment in the present. We begin to believe the wrong things. We believe that we'll never be greater than our greatest mistake. We don't verbally speak it. We live it. We refuse to allow ourselves to achieve the level of greatness to which God has called us.

We are called to embrace the miraculous work of Christ through our purpose. We are called to operate daily in the supernatural as we are led by the Spirit to do greater things. We are called to do what Christ did while He was on earth—and even greater things in His name so that the Father may be glorified (John 14:12–14). Unfortunately, far too many have failed to claim the inheritance this promise brings. Various past experiences that amble just within our faintest memories seem to resurface the moment a greater level of spiritual success is within our reach.

I once read that when two countries go to war, the victor takes the wealth of the losing nation to pay for expenses, and removes or destroys the religious artifacts and artwork to influence the culture. The victor takes one additional step to instill long-term change. The victor rewrites the history books in order to control the narrative of future generations. As time goes by, the rewritten history is believed and the future reflects it.

The same thing occurs on an individual basis. Your personal history can define your future. What you do, who you become, and what you believe about yourself is directly influenced by your past. While it is impossible for you to change your past, you can most certainly redeem it. Jesus takes the immovable past; sculpts the present using the scalpels of grace, empathy, and purpose; and presents a perfectly formed, healed, and freed version of you.

If we truly believed God knows all things, we wouldn't live in the shadow of the past. We would believe as William Carey, who declared, "The future is as bright as the promises of God."

Your future is bright. It's not bright because it's a reflection of your past. It's bright because it's a reflection of the Son. He knows everything about you, and He chooses you anyway.

WHO OWNS THE PAST?

When I read 1 Timothy 1:15, I can feel the burden Paul must have carried for him to say, "This is a faithful saying, and worthy of all acceptation, that Christ Jesus came into the world to save sinners; *of whom I am chief*" (NKJV, emphasis mine).

I'm fascinated by Paul's candor. The first part of the Scripture is so overwhelmingly encouraging, but it's the tagline at the end that reveals a depth to his battle. Paul is not aloof. He regretfully understands the suffering he caused others. I wonder if in his dreams, he saw the faces of the people he stoned. I wonder if Stephen's speech at martyrdom was set on repeat in his mind. I wonder if he felt compelled to do as much as he could to atone for his past mistakes, even though he had accepted God's gift of righteousness. I wonder if he vacillated as much as I do between feeling the need to earn redemption and find calm in the cross.

There is a profound difference between justification and sanctification. The moment we repent and accept Jesus as the Lord of our life, He declares us just. He stands between the judge and our sentence and declares that we are His. This is instantaneous, undeserved, and unexplainable. God immediately restores relationship, and while there may be consequences to our actions, the restoration is not to be earned but received. This is justification.

Sanctification is ongoing. It is the continual work of consecrating ourselves wholly to the Lord. You're not who you were, but you're not yet who you are going to be. Challenges arise when we confuse sanctification and justification. Whenever someone feels they need to earn their salvation, get cleaned up, or have a better track record before they walk in freedom and forgiveness, they have likely mixed up the two. It's symbolic of washing your hands, face, and body before taking a shower. Pointless.

John Piper adds:

> This is the rock where we stand when the dark clouds gather and the floods lick at our feet: justification is by grace alone (not mixed with our own merit), through faith alone (not mixed with our works), on the basis of Christ alone (not mingling his righteousness with ours, to the glory of God alone (not ours).

Depending on the depth of the past mistake, one may strive for years before positioning themselves to receive what God desired to give from the start. It's wasted time devoted to the past. How odd to think we would spend so much time in something so completely unchangeable. After all, you don't pray to alter the past. You pray to influence the present for the sake of the future.

In relation to time, we have three verb tenses: past tense, present tense, and future tense. Verb tenses tell us when an action is taking place. In the timeline of our lives, each tense has an owner. God owns the future, we own the present, but Satan owns the past. Think about it. Satan does not control your present, and he can't predict your future. All he can do is remind you of what you did, who you were, what you said, and why you should never be anything other than the crucible of your mistakes. The adversary attempts to alter our future through temptation in the present, but the reality is he cannot **force** us to do anything. This is the free-will gift we have been given.

Ah, but he is no fool. The Enemy understands the power of the past. He understands a simple reminder of your blunders can derail your present and negate your future. He has become a master storyteller. Unfortunately, the stories he tells are only half true. You **did** do that thing, say that word, hurt that person, ruin that relation-ship, get fired from that job, or worse.

Listening to the Enemy is like watching the first half of a sus-penseful movie. Every movie contains an initial incident that creates tension in the lives of the main characters. As the movie progresses, it reaches a climax, a pinnacle of chair-gripping intensity that locks you in. You know the resolution is coming; you just don't know how it will unfold. This is why you tune in, pay the money for movie tickets, and blow a small fortune on overpriced soda and popcorn.

The Enemy only shows the first half of the movie, then shuts it off. He's a jerk like that. He does this over and over again, only ever revealing the crisis, the mistake, the sorrow, and the shame. He never lets the story reach the point of redemption. We drift because we don't change the channel. We just keep watching the reruns of our past, and for many, this is a terrible TV show with dismal ratings.

If only you knew the rest of the story. If only you knew the immense value you hold within. If only you could see the end from the beginning, your worry would dissipate, your hope would rise, and you would walk in peace. Not because the problems would go away, but because you would know the ending.

Have you ever watched an intense movie a second time? Did you notice it didn't feel the same? In fact, you may spend more time watching the people around you who are watching the story for the first time, enjoying every reaction because you know how this particular movie ends.

It's no different in the world of sports. When my favorite teams are playing in a big game and I'm unable to watch it live, I don't want to know the score. I'd prefer to record the game and watch it later. Have you ever recorded a big game to view later, only to have someone tell you the outcome before you had a chance to watch it? If your team wins, even though you hate that someone revealed the final score, you're happy. If your team loses, and you're like me, you refuse to bother yourself with watching the game. Why expose yourself to such misery?

When you know the victorious outcome, you are able to watch the game with excitement and ease. It doesn't matter how bad things look; you know your team wins in the end. This is how God intends for us to live.

Yeah, I know what you're thinking. You don't know the end. But this isn't true. You don't know the *details* of the end. You know how your circumstance looks now. You know how good or bad it is in the moment, but you don't know what will come next, and believe it or not, that's okay. If we knew what came next, we would attempt to get there as quickly as possible and skip the process. It's the process that forms the person, not the end result.

It's our nature to draw from past experiences when we don't have a timeline for future promises. It's our nature to predict a hopeless future based on a hapless past. The past holds us captive more than we'd care to admit. When your thinking isn't rightly wired, it's difficult to process through unmet expectations, unguided dreams, and unwarranted hurts. The past has great sway over our lives.

In Revelation 12:10, Satan is described as the "accuser of our brothers" (ESV). Day and night he stands before Father God and accuses those whom the Father loves. What an impressive tactic. He heaps guilt, shame, regret, and hopelessness over what we are powerless to change. The Enemy will never accuse you based on your present acts of obedience. He will only bring up the past.

Even though God's mercies are new every morning (Lamentations 3:23), you may still be bound to a past moment. It doesn't matter if it's been one day or a thousand days since that regretful decision. It doesn't seem to matter how much good you've done since. It doesn't matter how many lives have been transformed, how many people you've helped, how many situations are better because of your simple acts of obedience. The accuser is never far behind, reminding you of the person "you really are." If you're not careful, you'll listen more intently to the playback of your mistakes than to your Father's declaration that you are more than your past.

TASTING THE PAST

Proverbs 26:11 is one of the more disturbing proverbs because of the imagery it incites. If you've ever owned a dog, the Scripture will resonate with you. Growing up, my parents owned a Lhasa Apso named Patches. She was a beautiful, spoiled, fun-loving dog, named after the patches of white hair on her otherwise brown coat. She was also the one who made this Scripture come alive for me. "Like a dog that returns to his vomit is a fool who repeats his folly" (ESV).

The first time I saw this proverb in action will forever be stamped on my mind. Patches had eaten too much and she began to vomit. What surprised me the most was how **quickly** she returned to the vomit. It was a matter of seconds, not minutes.

When you feel hopeless, you'll repeat the mistake. When you feel hapless, you'll revisit the mistake. Neither one is healthy. Perhaps the reason you have not pressed forward is because you keep returning to your folly. You may not be hungry for a fruitful present or a hopeful future because you are still feasting on your past.

The Enemy knows a truth that we would be wise to learn: **Failure is a moment, not a person.** You may return to your past for the education, but nobody likes to repeat a grade. According to Henry Ford, "Failure is simply the opportunity to begin again, this time more intelligently." You can't allow yourself to begin again while being tethered to the past.

For a season, my friend allowed his past infidelity to dictate his present and define his future. It's a familiar story, and likely one you've read before. He has since moved forward—reluctantly, painfully, but forward nonetheless. He is not driftwood. He decided to take control of his life, re-engage with God, confront his demons, and work toward healing.

There is a collection of ill-wishing people who would fatefully predict how my friend's marriage would end. They would do so based on statistics, experience, or bitterness. In this instance, they'd be wrong. My friend and his wife have since had another child and they are growing and healing more and more each day. It's because he decided to make a firm commitment to becoming the man God calls him to be and finding peace in his righteousness.

He's not there yet, but he's better than he was. Maybe it's time for you to settle your yesterdays and discover, once again, the hope God has for your future.

SAME PERSON, DIFFERENT SHAPE

I admit to being at a disadvantage because I don't know your circumstance, who has hurt you, how you've self-destructed, or what event has marred your ambition and self-confidence. None of those things affect God's ability to redeem your past, but they do affect your ability to relinquish your grip on the past.

The greater the offense, pain, or emotional trauma, the longer it takes for our finite minds to attribute the justice we demand to the Lord, or break its control over our thoughts.

The hang-up when dealing with our pasts is our desire to return to something which no longer exists. We aim to be the person we used to be, with the peace we used to have, in a place we can't return to. Once you encounter pain, you will never be the same. God heals, but the memories and the scars remain. This inevitable realization carries with it depression and despondency. In short, you stop trying because "things will never be the same."

Embrace that realization. Own it, because different does not mean defeat. You can craft the realization you choose to live in. You are the bottle that forces the water to conform to its shape. The water does not resist the shape of the bottle, no matter how large, small, awkward, unique, or mundane the vessel may be. As your soul is healed and redeemed, your personality, attitude, and outlook will fit the path of the Spirit.

So, acknowledge the past. Don't pretend it never happened. How has it reshaped you? What attributes of this new shape do you not desire? Where do you need God to re-form you? This new shape will eventually become your new normal, and that's okay. Through every trial you've never been "less than," no matter how others may have treated you.

Your new shape becomes beautiful to those around you as you allow it to form by the promptings of Holy Spirit. The previous shape may not have been attractive to some, but is now irresistible to others. Your new shape is a new ministry. Your new shape will change new lives. What the Enemy fails to understand is although he destroys who you used to be, God makes all things new and uses it for a greater purpose. Your past did not destroy you or you wouldn't be reading this book. Embrace your new shape as water embraces a new container and allow God to flow through the new you.

As I think about this reshaping, I think about what Jesus endured. The beating, scourging, mocking, and torture completely deconstructed His frame and soul, but the resurrection birthed a glorified body. He still had the scars, but He did not stagger. He had the memories but with greater moxie. Instead of walking in fear and defeat, He was more invincible than ever.

If it didn't kill you, you are stronger. If it didn't completely destroy you, you are braver. You are wiser. You are kinder. You are more empathetic. Everything the Enemy meant for your destruction has simply created a greater, more impenetrable form, and God is now filling that form with purpose, vision, and life.

As you allow the Holy Spirit to re-form you, there may be an uncanny development. You may begin to be thankful for your past, not drift because of it.

THREE

. . . .

THE INTENTION DRIFT

In the late-1980s, Kareem Abdul-Jabbar strolled down the center aisle of my elementary school auditorium in Salem, New Jersey. At least, that's who I thought it was at first glance. It was a typical elementary school assembly, set to discourage drug use and encourage good grades. My best friend, Wesley, and I sat together. I chose the seat at the end of the row.

The individual leading the assembly had invited several "famous people" to come speak to this rowdy crowd of second and third graders. His plan was to show how these celebrities would **not** have been successful had they used drugs. This was at the height of the "Just Say No" political campaign driven by First Lady Nancy Reagan.

The interviewer played to the crowd. We had no idea what famous person decided to speak with us that day. In an eruption of convincing flair, he exclaimed, "Would you please welcome Kareem Abdul-Jabbar!"

I couldn't believe it! Kareem Abdul-Jabbar! In my school! I whipped around just in time to see an incredibly tall black man wearing a Los Angeles Lakers uniform and sports goggles walk by me. Me, of all people! I was so excited, I blurted out, "It's him!"

My friend corrected me. "No, it's not," he insisted in a loud whisper.

Trying to save face, I responded, "Not! I meant it's *not* him!" I was only eight years old, and I guess my sports acumen was still undeveloped. To be honest, I wasn't sure what Kareem Abdul-Jabbar even looked like. I just assumed it was him because he was tall and dressed like a Los Angeles Laker.

Of course, I now realize the silliness of the assumption. There is no way the six-time NBA Champion, nineteen-time All-Star, six-time NBA MVP Kareem Abdul-Jabbar would come to Mannington Township School in Salem, New Jersey, to give a motivational anti-drug speech to a bunch of second and third graders. The man I saw was a counterfeit. He dressed the part and looked the part, but did not live the part. There is only one Kareem Abdul-Jabbar, and this guy was not him.

This happened over thirty years ago, but I still remember being disappointed. I felt scammed. I remember thinking, *if you're going to make the effort to throw a school assembly, at least get the real deal.* Slackers.

People still crave the real deal. They can spot a fraud in a New York minute. Authenticity has more relational value per capita than any other trait, especially in leadership. One of my favorite podcasts is the Craig Groeschel Leadership podcast. At the end of each episode, he signs off with a statement I absolutely love: "Be yourself. People would rather follow a leader who is always real than one who is always right." It's no secret or profound revelation that this generation values what is real, true, and unaltered. Unfortunately, this generation is also surrounded by misrepresentation.

It is estimated that a millennial will take nearly twenty-five thousand selfies in their lifetime. That equates to just under one selfie per day. To date, one thousand selfies are posted to Instagram every second, with 68 percent of posters admitting to editing their selfies before posting. In other words, nearly 3.5 out of 5 pictures you see have been altered in some way. Few would call their photo editing a deceptive practice, but the result is a deceived consumer on a global scale. We have created a culture of morbid comparison, but we are comparing wax figures. Whoever sculpts the greatest life wins. The losers gather the useless clay in an attempt to capture something resembling beauty from the remains. The outcome is a generation whose identity has been fractured and frayed with an increased potential for self-harm.

Jamie Ducharme of *Time* magazine writes:

There's been a marked uptick in so-called deaths of despair—those involving drugs, alcohol or suicide—among millennials over the last decade, according to a new report released by public-health groups Trust for America's Health and Well Being Trust. Drug, alcohol and suicide deaths have risen in nearly every age group over the last decade, but the increase has been especially pronounced for younger Americans. Between 2007 and 2017, drug-related deaths increased by 108% among adults ages 18 to 34, while alcohol-related deaths increased by 69% and suicides increased by 35%, according to the report, which drew on Centers for Disease Control and Prevention data. Altogether, about 36,000 millennials died "deaths of despair" in 2017, with fatal drug overdoses being the biggest driver.

In a separate article, the same author also notes:

The research, conducted by health insurer Cigna and the market research firm Ipsos, found that young people ages 18 to 22 are the most likely to be lonely. Loneliness is a major threat to Americans' mental, physical and emotional well-being and can have huge consequences for public health, given the well-researched connections between loneliness and health issues ranging from substance abuse to heart disease.

The avenues of connectivity are greater than any other time in history, yet young adults are lonelier than ever before. They live in a world of unrelenting social comparison. Studies are continuing to reveal a direct correlation between social media usage and mental illness, depression, anxiety, and suicide.

But this chapter is not on the dangers of social media, faux connectivity, shallow relationships, or wax figures. It's about intention.

When God crafted you, He did so with your designation in mind. He formed within you purpose and destiny, and He branded you with love and intentionality. You are everything He wants you to be, and you are everything to Him. You're His favorite son, His favorite daughter, and He never stops thinking about you. You're not flawed in His eyes, because when He looks at you, He sees more than a body. He sees soul and spirit, both constructed with faultless care. You are His prized creation, and as Bob Goff so accurately accounts, "God never compares what He creates."

But we are not God. We compare. A lot.

Our self-involved culture can take any trait you possess and make it atrocious. If you're too tall, you'll hear about it. If you're too short, you'll hear about it. If you are average height, you'll hear about it, because who wants to be average? Spend a few minutes online and you'll feel bad about your hair, complexion, make-up, weight, height, speaking ability, influence, smile, face, nails, clothes, leadership, family, and more.

The world is buried in comparison. My friend Darren Hileman once coined the axiom, "If you compare and compete, you'll live in defeat. You'll either feel superior or inferior. Either way, you lose." Comparison will always place you in an unhealthy headspace. Comparison is a symptom of fallen humanity. We see it with Cain and Abel. Would Cain have felt slighted if there was no Abel? Comparison yielded envy and envy led to murder. After all, sometimes it's easier to kill your brother than alter your offering.

THE REAL YOU

God's intention is for you to be you. There are no exceptions. Everyone plays a role in the kingdom of God, and your success will be determined by how well you play your role. You could play an incredible Aaron Burr in the musical *Hamilton*, but the accolades won't come if you were supposed to play Alexander Hamilton. You will be rewarded on how well you carried out what God called *you* to do.

In a misguided effort to become the person others think we should be, we drift. We slowly craft a counterfeit version of ourselves, not to please God but to please the flawed around us. Ironically, playing someone else may bring great earthly success but eternal poverty. God will never bless a counterfeit version of you or me.

The frustration will arise when you attempt to live life in someone else's skin. You will be pulled off course and haunted by the relentless feeling that something is missing. Not only will you get lost in this internal conflict, but your grip on joy will loosen. You will find yourself simply existing, doing what everyone else thinks you should do instead of finding joy in your designed destiny. What do you do when you're not sure of God's intention for your life? You'll either focus on the meaningless or do nothing at all.

Yet kingdom obedience does not anguish over results. If you are walking in faith, the results are up to God, not you. After all, if we could do it on our own, why would we need God? He is not formulaic, and He is not predictable. He is God and we are not, so leave the results to Him and focus all your attention on obedience.

With that being said, I must ask a few questions: Who are you? What have you believed about yourself that simply is not true? How have you compared yourself to others? Did it make you feel inferior or superior? Who has God crafted you to become, and what is He calling you to do?

Perhaps you love starting new ventures, trying new things, meeting new people, and accepting new challenges. Perhaps you're the kind of guy or girl who will start a business, but after it's up and running, you'll hand it off for someone else to maintain. Maybe you are perfectly content sitting in a cubicle all day processing spreadsheets. Maybe you're excellent at managing someone else's vision. However, God made you, He made you with intention, and He can't wait for you to be you.

WATCHES AND TRENCH COATS

I'll never forget the first time I went to New York City. I was amazed at the scope, stature, and intensity of the city. It was so much bigger than I had imagined. I arrived on a tour bus with some friends. As I stepped off the bus I was immediately greeted by a man in a trench coat. He wasted no time opening that coat and revealing rows of "authentic" Rolex watches for only $20. What a bargain! Of course, I bought one.

Yes, I knew it wasn't real (although secretly, I hoped he had put the real thing in his coat by mistake). A few hours later a pin on the watch band fell out and I never wore that watch again.

Thinking back on that experience, I realized something significant about the fake watches in the street salesman's coat. There were no replicas of cheap watches. Every watch mimicked greatness. They were replicas of the most expensive watches you could buy. He had everything from Patek Philippe to Rolex to Breitling, but no Casio.

The Enemy does not possess the ability to create, but he does have the ability to counterfeit. The role of the counterfeiter is not to make an item opposite of the original. No, the counterfeiter wants to make something as close to the original as possible, and if he is going to counterfeit something, he's going to clone what's expensive, valuable, and longed for.

Since our adversary can't create a person, he attempts to mis-create them. He convinces us that a better life is available, we just have to take a bite of the apple.

The enemy will always try to convince you there is an easier way with a lower personal cost. He doesn't want you to be yourself because your "self" is laced with destiny and power. Instead, he'll lead you to believe your best parts are your worst parts, and the only way you can succeed is to be someone else.

We drift when we start to believe we must become someone else to be valuable. Our misaligned thoughts become a self-fulfilling prophecy, and the comparison game buries us in inadequacy and insecurity. You will always feel hopeless when you try to live someone else's life.

FOMO

In the words of my friend Melinda, "God don't make junk." Even with full revelation of that reality, we find ourselves doubting Him and His plan. We lose faith in the purity of His intention. Fear that we don't measure up or will never find happiness and success sparks us to change, but not all change is good or worth doing.

We may not admit it, but we fear a lot of things. Some fear spiders, some fear heights, some fear darkness. We surrender control to the things we fear. We give authority to those items, whether it be snakes or flowers, to position us in a perpetual state of panic and fear. But we weren't born with fear; it was downloaded to our internal hard drive as we grew and experienced the ups and downs of life. The things we fear we must constantly strive to overcome, to condition ourselves to no longer be afraid. In doing so we reclaim our authority. This is easy to write, harder to live. For many, their greatest fear is the fear of missing out, otherwise known as FOMO.

You can only fear missing out if you believe the lie that God has no intention for you to experience joy or success. It's amazing to me that followers of Jesus believe He died for their sins, was raised from the dead, ascended into heaven, and now sits at the right hand of Father God interceding for us, but we can't believe He didn't make a mistake in choosing us. We place more faith in our flaws than His preferred future.

To make things worse, Satan never stops whispering doubt: What if God *isn't* good? What if He changed His mind about you? What if that thing you did disqualified you from ever walking in grace again? You know why he left you. You know why she left you. You know why your kids won't return your call. You know you'll never get the promotion. You know your boss hates you. You know everyone talks about you when you're not around. You're a terrible friend. You call yourself a leader? You actually think God would honor you after what you've done? Maybe it's time for you to stop being yourself and be someone else.

After all, you know you'll Never. Be. Enough.

Every word Satan speaks drives fear into your psyche, like a stake into the heart of hope. It's demonic, and it works. He understands you'll be spiritually castrated if he can affect your view of yourself and your view of Father God. Fear is demonic, and it's the Enemy's way of twisting your perception of God's intention.

The intention drift is horribly difficult to correct because it is cyclical in nature. You see a flaw, doubt God cared when He made you, and try to be someone else, only to fail at that too. You think you tried to mimic the wrong person, so you try again, and with each metamorphosis gone wrong, you move further from the identity God imprinted upon your frame. God will never honor a decision made from fear, because He is not the God of fear. He is the God of faith.

But what about the fear of the Lord, which we are encouraged to have? Isn't that supposed to lead to wisdom, not condemnation? Too many people misinterpret these Scriptures. You're to fear the Lord, not be afraid of the Lord. Let me explain.

When I was in my mid-twenties, I went to Las Vegas for the first time with some of my closest friends. One night before dinner, we decided to walk around a boutique shopping plaza even though we clearly could not afford to buy even their least-expensive items.

As the five of us walked into a well-known boutique jewelry store, I decided to brazenly ask to try on one of their watches. The clerk must have felt sorry for me. He smiled, grabbed some white gloves and a cloth, and gently removed the watch from its case. In my naïveté, I assumed the watch would cost three or four thousand dollars. I was way off. As I carefully draped the Cartier watch over my wrist, I asked the gentleman, "How much does this baby cost?" It was a valid question since it didn't have the typical price tag found in department store jewelry cases. I never really gripped the profound meaning of the statement "If you have to ask..." until that moment.

"Thirty-thousand dollars," he replied.

I don't think I can accurately explain the heat wave that came over me at that moment. I was suddenly quite fearful. People watching me must have thought someone hit the slow-motion button in my brain, because I don't think I ever treated anything so carefully. In that moment, I was wearing something on my wrist that was more expensive than a brand-new car. I was scared of doing anything that would damage this majestic creation of gold and diamonds.

I slowly removed the watch, gave it back to the jewelry barista, and took a few steps back. I didn't stop smiling all day, and I couldn't wait to tell people about the ridiculously expensive watch I had placed on my wrist.

This is the fear of the Lord. It's a mindset that refuses to do anything that would damage the connection we have with Him. We allow so many God blockers to enter our eye gate and ear gate, then wonder why we can't seem to hear His voice or we struggle to pray. We abuse His grace and neglect His mercy. We think we can treat Him however we please and He'll simply crawl back to us like a well-disciplined puppy. Not only is this not who God is, it's also a terrible relationship ideology.

I don't fear the wrath of my earthly father. It's not because he doesn't have the power to correct or the strength to enforce discipline. It's because I know his heart is not to punish. He wants to build up and celebrate my successes. He desires to see me achieve my dreams and God's calling on my life. Even though my earthly father is not perfect, I hate the idea of ever doing anything that would cause him to feel anything but pride for me.

Let's bring this full circle. When we don't know the truth about Father God, we fail to understand His intention for us. When we don't understand this intention, we think He made a mistake in creating us. When we think we are a mistake, less than, or missing the components that make a person great, we become fearful.

Fear causes us to take matters into our own hands and craft a version of ourselves that would please Him, all the while distorting His creation in the process. We lose sight of our calling and our purpose and begin living someone else's life. I'm not talking about the life of our neighbor, friend, or favorite movie star. No, we begin living the life the adversary has lured us to live. It's a life that closely resembles Christ since we are made in His image, but it's no Rolex. It will eventually fall apart, and we'll long to throw it in the trash just like my street-corner purchase.

This can be an uncomfortable realization, especially for believers. While we certainly cannot claim authority over God, we condition ourselves to not fear Him. We attempt to lose ourselves in His love, and we forget about His might and His righteous right hand. We thank Him for His grace and ignore the future call of judgment. If we are honest, we often fear debt, divorce, and death more than the divine.

Time and time again we condition ourselves to ignore His ability, and His right, to call us into account for our sins while quoting verses about His mercy. We associate fear with the bad and boldness with the good, but the fear of God isn't a bad thing. It's the fear of the Lord that causes us to put our trust in Him. If we truly fear God, we acknowledge His power, and the acknowledgement of His power should lead us to fear nothing else at all. I believe it is this simple realization that motivated Paul to exhort, "Be anxious for nothing" (Philippians 4:6 NKJV).

As you seek His face and quiet the voice of the Enemy, something beautiful emerges: the true intentions of the One who created you. He is the perfect Father who desires to empower you in your calling, not imprison you in comparison. He wants to take all of you and fashion you into something valuable.

Great artists make great art out of driftwood and *you* are His greatest work.

FOUR

THE SUCCESS DRIFT

One of the unexpected catalysts of drifting is success. Success will inevitably change us, but the change doesn't have to be negative. Yet, if God wants us to succeed, why does success seem to be so detrimental to our calling?

Success, like money, is a magnifier of what is seated deep in the heart of humanity. For some, success brings them even closer to the intangibles. They withdraw into their families for solace and refuse to let themselves be subjected to the lure and trappings of this world. For others, success is the result of a life lived well and the fruit they bear is a lasting legacy of lives changed.

Success is not a bad thing. Success in the hand of a heart humbled before God will change the world. Success in an unchecked heart leaves a wake of broken vessels. At the core of un-

65

tamed success is abused ambition. In fact, James declares where you find selfish ambition, you find every evil practice (James 3:14–16).

It would appear selfishness is the impetus of every destructive act. Pride, selfishness, and envy all have a common trait. They all find their vitality through an overemphasis of self. Success can cause you to overemphasize your ways, your logic, your will, and your demands. Success can cause you to diminish the accomplishments of your team to ensure you stay on top. It will tempt you to degrade and derail while disguising your carnage as aspiration.

You may not have started out as a self-serving egotist, but success has a funny way of morphing us into the worst version of ourselves. Ask King David. Ask Solomon. Ask Saul. Ask any number of leaders, both Christian and other, who scaled the mountain of success only to trip over their own ego at the apex.

So what does the **success drift** look like? How do you know if you're successful yet drifting away from who God has called you to become? While there may certainly be more causes than what I'm listing, here are five tripping points that often convert success into failure and cause us to drift.

TRIPPING POINT #1: MISNAMED SUCCESS

As a follower of Jesus, success is defined by obedience. One can succeed in many different areas, but if we are not obedient to the Lord, our successes are worth very little. The apostle Paul counted everything as loss when compared to knowing God more and sharing in His suffering (Philippians 3:8–10). If you call success anything other than obedience to God, you'll run the risk of misaligning your priorities. You'll elect to serve success at the expense of your family, relationships, and health.

We attach heavy words to these misguided strivings. We claim our success is really about "security," "purpose," and maybe even "our calling." We misname success in an attempt to lessen the severity of its venom, yet the Scriptures are clear. Whoever loves money never has enough. Those who love wealth are never satisfied with their income (Ecclesiastes 5:10). In other words, the desire for success is unquantifiable and insatiable.

You can label selfish ambition however you'd like, but if it causes you to drift, you can't call it success. Ultimately, your success is not *your* success, it's His. If ever you are misled to believe you "deserve" what you have, or somehow through your own efforts you've achieved your specific level of success, beware.

King Saul is one who never understood proper success. He measured success by the victories won, the size of his army, and the expanse of his kingdom. He's morally confusing, yet I'm intrigued by him. When we speak of blown leadership potential, we must simply turn to 1 Samuel to see Saul certainly deserves the negative press he's received. Many church leaders today use his life as a stark example of how *not* to behave, yet I would assume many of us operate this way.

We're impatient. We're impulsive. We're compromising. We're paranoid. We're liars.

Yet...

We're warriors. We're compassionate. We're esteeming. We're persistent. We're more than conquerors.

Our success is the culmination of past mistakes and future promises that ball themselves up into a sphere of personal confusion which, if left unbridled, will build into an assemblage of self-destructive behavior. A pocket full of dynamite can create a large crater, and our pockets are lined with moral explosives.

Saul's explosive tendencies placed him in a provincial purgatory. It's a torturous state where the haunting of what could have been collides with the reality of what is. The decisions born out of the collision of past and present never benefit the future. Saul held on to his understanding of success. The quandary is, God allowed it. Beware, my friend, as God may allow you to retain your position as He raises up your replacement.

If Saul had a greater level of self-awareness, he would have invested in David, not attempted to murder him. He would have trained him to exalt him, not chase him to bury him. Had Saul looked to exalt, educate, and expand David's influence, his leadership would have been modeled this day. Unfortunately, he allowed the spiritual gifts of another to nullify his own anointing.

Saul had received the prophetic word from Samuel. He squandered his opportunity, was disobedient to the Lord far too many times, and the kingdom would soon be ripped from his hands and given to another. It was clear. It was irrefutable. Yet, somehow in the pride of position, Saul determined his success was not God's to take away, so he stayed. He failed to understand how far he had drifted.

After a myriad of poor choices, Saul was pursuing David at Keilah, seeking to kill him for being, of all things, honorable and loyal: "Saul was told that David had gone to Keilah, and he said, 'God has delivered him into my hands, for David has imprisoned himself by entering a town with gates and bars'" (1 Samuel 23:7).

This was not the case at all. God was actually delivering David and detaining Saul. Somewhere along the line, Saul's pride caused him to suffer from a severe case of mistaken identity. Despite God's prophetic proclamation, despite Samuel's rebuke, and despite David's honor and heroics, Saul was determined to prove God was still on his side. Saul was seeking to kill an innocent man at all costs, and somehow he believed it was the Lord who would allow it to happen. Saul was operating in his calling, but David by His anointing. To the outside observer, Saul appeared to be successful and David appeared to be the forsaken. Anointing and favor are often disguised as humility and passivity.

Pride-filled leadership can cause such a blindness. Stephen Covey noted, "We judge ourselves by our intentions and others by their behavior." We often mistake talent for presence and results for anointing. We fail to realize that our talent can take us where our character can't keep us, and this was the case with Saul. We are far too quick to elevate capacity over character and wonder why the structure splinters in the storm.

We misname earthy achievement as success and mistakenly confuse our success in the past for anointing in the present. The antidote to this poisonous way of thinking is found in His presence. We must come prostrate, broken, desperate before the Lord each day and proclaim His promises, prepare for forgiveness, and plan for restoration. We must never assume because He was on our side in our former triumphs, He will delay judgment for latter disobedience.

Saul thought God was still fighting for him, yet God had moved on and anointed a man who would carry out his promises. David was obviously not without flaw, but the Lord's favor is drawn to a repentant heart. The Scriptures declare, "Whoever conceals his transgressions will not prosper, but he who confesses and forsakes them will obtain mercy" (Proverbs 28:1 ESV) and "If we confess our sins, he is faithful and just to forgive us our sins and to cleanse us from all unrighteousness" (1 John 1:9 ESV). David wasn't perfect, but His heart was to please God, and despite his surroundings, he found success.

Success is momentary, and if left unchecked will always drift toward failure. If you're unsure whether you associate more closely with Saul than David, look for indicators.

For example, I do a great deal of premarital counseling. One of the common caution flags in young, star-struck couples is unrealistic expectations. While they may not admit it, many believe marriage will be an unending euphoric state of bliss. They emphatically declare divorce is not an option, and I applaud the sentiment. They are insistent their marriage will succeed, and minstrels will sing songs of their splendor. Anyone who has ever experienced marriage understands their level of delusion and how unrealistic these expectations are. Success early in the relationship is never an indicator of how the relationship will endure.

The unrealistic expectation of those who have experienced success is that they'll never fail again. Believing this lie will cause you to do everything you can to prevent the fall, only to magnify the possibility. Most successful people will flaunt their failure freely, understanding failure is what formed them to be successful. Yet many don't believe that formula should endure. Once successful, always successful. This is the lie they've believed. It's the lie Saul believed, and ultimately it was the lie David believed which caused him to drift, have an affair with Bathsheba, and murder her husband.

What brings success in one season can deliver failure in another. When you can define success as obedience, you'll understand that success is contradistinctive depending on the season. I wonder if the apostle Paul felt successful after being beaten and imprisoned. I wonder if he felt successful when shipwrecked and stoned. I would argue he felt quite successful inasmuch as his suffering was the result of great obedience. For Paul, success wasn't stuff, it was submission. As long as your expectations are shackled to God's will, you will be successful. Live independent of His Word and you will certainly drift, and one day your kingdom will be taken away from you as well. If you do not anticipate future trials, temptations, or tempests, you'll likely drift in your leadership, or worse, seek to manipulate and control others to avoid future pain and disappointment.

TRIPPING POINT #2: UNDEFINED ASSIGNMENT

If you don't know what God is asking you to do, your days will become clouded with all the wrong tasks. As a kid, were you ever asked to clean your room? It's all your parent or guardian wanted. Clean your room. You could have vacuumed the living room, swept the kitchen, and done the dishes, and still been unsuccessful. It's not that your activity was bad; it was just wrong. You were disobedient and, if done intentionally, also rebellious.

One morning my father texted me some thoughts circling in his head, and they resonated with my spirit. He shared:

We are, of course, creatures who if left to ourselves, would promote ourselves without any reference to God or preference for Him. It is easy for us to jump headfirst and headstrong into what we perceive to be important activity **for** Him without taking time **with** Him. Our silent and disguised rebellion articulates with decisions and actions a life which would seemingly repel us from the still small voice desiring to dictate his will.

It was far too deep a statement so early in the morning, but powerful, nonetheless. We can be quite active and yet quite disobedient in the kingdom. He may call us to pause, yet in His name we press on nonetheless. Kingdom progress from carnal pursuit will never please the Lord. He will not allow our disobedience to spoil the fruit, but it will affect our favor and anointing.

The Enemy likes to deceive us in this way. If he can't keep us from heaven, he'll keep us busy. He'll tie us up doing all the wrong things so we never fulfill the purpose God has for us. Perhaps God has called you to be a missionary, yet you have chosen to be active in the local church, lead a small group, and engage in weekly street evangelism. It's not that you are doing anything bad, but you have become disobedient by focusing on everything else but what God has called you to do.

If you have not received a defined assignment from the Lord, it's time to start seeking Him. The last thing you want is to be successful in things that don't matter. Not everyone is going to be a pastor, missionary, or evangelist. You may operate as a pastor when God is calling you to be an entrepreneur. You will always be happier and more fulfilled when you walk in obedience to Him, despite what you envision for yourself.

If you *have* received your assignment from the Lord, follow through. Success doesn't mean it will be easy. It can be quite hard and yet quite fulfilling. You may even find yourself echoing James' exhortation to "count it all joy...when you meet trials" (James 1:2 ESV).

Recently I heard the story of a woman in Asia whose goal was to get arrested for sharing the gospel. She was bothered that she had not suffered in this way, like many who had gone before her. When she was finally arrested and thrown in prison, she rejoiced. Some would say she must have lost her mind. I say she had a kingdom understanding of success. Success, to the Lord, may look like foolishness to others, but if it always made sense, there would be no need for faith. Make sure your success is sanctified or you may end up flaunting your disobedience, expecting a reward but receiving the rod.

TRIPPING POINT #3: UNACCEPTED ACCOUNTABILITY

Accountability is sticky and ugly and hard, but it's also necessary. Not everyone needs to know your stuff, but someone does, because every deceptive act begins with a small concession. When you don't understand success, you:

- Intentionally report inaccurate numbers to make yourself look good.
- Justify the charge on the company credit card as a business expense.
- Rationalize that it was only a single lunch with a member of the opposite sex—no harm, no foul. Besides, it was work related.
- Clock in and sit in the employee break room for another thirty minutes.

- Take a sick day but don't record it.
- Have intimate conversations with someone other than your spouse and say they are just a friend.
- View pornography under the guise that it's not hurting anyone.

In order to maintain success, you'll need accountability. It's not that you have the intention to drift, but every successful person who removes themselves from accountability is an easy target for the one who wants nothing more than to steal, kill, and destroy you.

I don't know what areas are stumbling blocks for you, but invite someone into your story and allow them to ask the hard questions. If you're looking for someone to be accountable to, I recommend finding someone who fulfills the following:

- They are older than you, much older if possible. They have likely been where you are and know the way out.
- They are of the same gender. Don't give temptation a foothold. If you struggle with a same-sex attraction, be sure to ask someone whom you deem safe.
- They are trustworthy. This is often built on time and reputation. Look for someone who has a pattern of trustworthiness. Chances are, if they are older, they have little to gain by sharing your struggles.
- They are kingdom minded. Do they want you to succeed because they understand God's promise and calling on your life?
- You drive the relationship. You set the agenda and you schedule the face time. If they are worth asking to be a mentor, coach, or accountability partner, they likely main-

tain an active life. Don't expect them to cater their schedule to yours. You make the effort to make it happen.

- If you're unaccountable, you're drifting, no matter how much evidence you bring to the contrary.

TRIPPING POINT #4: UNCLEAR VISION

Many who achieve a level of success do so because they possessed a clear vision of what they were motivated to accomplish. Far too many lack vision for the next phase, so they attempt to duplicate past successes using past processes, but the old wineskin cannot contain the new wine. It bursts, spilling promise and potential everywhere. People then spend a majority of their effort striving to restore past glory rather than attain new vision.

Be sure you have a clear vision. Vision empowers you to say *no* to really good ideas because you see something greater, but if you don't *see* it before you *see* it, you'll never *see* it. This vision should not conflict with the Lord's perfect plan for your life so it would be wise to seek Him before exterior counsel. God advised Jeremiah to gather his vision from the mouth of the Lord, not from the prophetic voices around him (Jeremiah 23:16). I'd advise you to do the same. You'll find He has already created a future which aligns with your passions. He knows, after all, because he made you.

TRIPPING POINT #5: UNGUARDED AMBITION

Successful people are ambitious. Ambition on its own is not a negative trait. We don't often view ambition or promotion as an evil or rebellious thing. But we are inundated with the general population's view of personal ambition as a good thing, with little consideration of God's ambition for humanity. A great deal of danger comes alongside selfish ambition. It promotes the prosperity of self over the health of others. Instead of expressing concern over the spiritual condition of the people around you, we leverage their shortcomings to endorse our strengths.

In the Gospel of John, Jesus is recorded saying, "I do not accept glory from human beings, but I know you. I know that you do not have the love of God in your hearts. I have come in my Father's name, and you do not accept me; but if someone else comes in his own name, you will accept him. How can you believe since you accept glory from one another but do not seek the glory that comes from the only God?" (John 5:41–44).

Jesus makes a distinct and fascinating correlation between self-promotion and God's love. As we long to promote ourselves, we may find ourselves in a loveless relationship with God—a relationship that values the praise of others over the declarations of God. Love for God results in us bearing a towel to serve, not a sword to slay. Selfish ambition would discard the towel as a useless weapon, and instead pick up the arsenal of personal preference, armed to the teeth with every strategy bent on transmitting the image of self-promotion and aggressive independence.

Sometimes it's the headstrong and head-first who find themselves arriving at their desired destination the quickest, though the destination may not always be found in Christ. Success isn't a bad thing, but the pride associated with success will cause us to value projects over people. We'll drift, not intentionally yet exponentially, away from God's gentle nudge. You may find great success, but at a price God never intended for you to pay.

SUCCESS SELF-ASSESSMENT

What questions can we ask to ensure our ambitions line up with God's? What actions—true and right actions—can we perform to ensure we find ourselves embracing and encouraging God's ambitions for humanity?

I. Does This Decision Exalt Christ?

In the desire to achieve, we toss our relational scraps to Christ as if He were a beggar who would be lucky to dine off our leftovers. Whatever action you're about to do, whatever scheme is in your mind, does it exalt the compassionate and redemptive person of Christ or does it exalt your brand?

II. Does This Action Draw Others to His Kingdom?

When others see you, do they see the drawbridge firmly closed and the moat filled with flesh-eating alligators? Or do they see an open invitation to the greatest afterparty known to man? If our actions repel people from relationship, chances are we are acting selfishly. If they draw people into a relationship with God because they see Christ in us, then chances are we are acting copiously benevolent.

III. Will I Regret This Decision in the Future?

You may not believe in regret, you may not think about regret, but at the end of our lives when we stand before our God, I firmly believe we will experience regret. Regret will be found in those moments we didn't listen to His voice. Moments when we followed the common sense of others instead of the divine sense of

God. So, before you take a step, ask yourself, *is this something I will regret? Will my family suffer? Will this harm my marriage? Will this damage my integrity?* Remember, each of us are called to carry the cross of Christ, but we must carry it His way.

HEALTHY SUCCESS AND THE FULFILLMENT MYTH

So, what does healthy success look like? It begins with a foundational understanding that God doesn't make you successful exclusively for personal joy, although there may be great joy attached to your achievements.

Healthy success is living every day in humble obedience to Him. The world will incessantly bombard you with an alternative theory. It will seek to convince you of the necessity of power, fame, influence, and wealth. It will celebrate your eighty-hour work weeks only to condemn you for your failed marriage and broken relationships. History is littered with high-achieving people who appeared to have it all yet took their lives in the end. It's exhausting, chasing after the wind. They never found what they needed. They never found Jesus.

I want you to experience healthy success. Healthy success is selfless, shared with others, and always points to Jesus. We are simply a conduit in which God blesses so that we can be a blessing. We are successful to help others succeed. You'll not drift in your success if you remember it's all about Him.

FIVE

....

THE SIN DRIFT

About a decade ago, I took a handful of students to New York City to break them out of their comfort zone and introduce them to an eclectic spiritual dynamic. We stayed at a group home in Brooklyn. It was an organization that prided itself on taking the physically, emotionally, and spiritually crippled and, with God's help, guiding them toward wholeness. We sat in a circle on our first night, hearing a stream of stories from the men and women who had found Jesus, turned their lives around, and were striving to walk in freedom one day at a time.

I only remember one story from that night. It broke my heart in so many ways, and even more so when I became a father. I don't remember her name, but she was an attractive young lady with blonde hair. Her face was aged far beyond her years, and even though she had been forgiven and had committed her life to Christ, she was learning how to hope again despite her brokenness. She spoke softly at first, but as she continued her voice rose, an emotional concoction of confidence, conviction, and regret.

"I never thought I could do what I did," she said. "I was a popular girl in high school. I was the prom queen and my husband was the prom king. We had a storybook life. We got married shortly after we graduated high school. He was making really good money and we were comfortable. We even had a couple of kids. I don't know why I started, but I began using cocaine."

She paused for a moment to collect herself. I'm not sure how long she had been in this Christian rehabilitation program, but she clearly hadn't shared this story often. The others had rehearsed their testimony and had their delivery down, but this young lady's words seemed so raw. "I thought I had it under control. I was wrong. I didn't realize I had a problem until it was too late. My husband found out and he cut me off financially. I became desperate to use again..."

This time when she paused, she lowered her head. Tears streamed down her cheeks, her voice broke, and she struggled to put her thoughts into words. "I didn't have money anymore so I...um...I...I sold my kids. I sold my kids into prostitution."

I couldn't believe what I was hearing. I couldn't help but cry with her. My heart was crushed, thinking what she must have endured on her way to Jesus' redemption.

She continued, "If you had told me as a high school senior I would grow up to have so much but throw it all away because of drugs, I would have laughed at you. If you would have told me then I'd sell my kids for money, I may have hit you. I don't know how it happened."

Whenever I think of this young lady, I pray she's doing well. I pray she's been reunited with her family and that God has supernaturally healed them and restored their marriage. Sin took root in her life and she drifted. She drifted away from everything she ever wanted to become and loathed everything she became.

In James 1:14–15, we are warned of this demonic progression: *"But each person is tempted when he is lured and enticed by his own desire. Then desire when it has conceived gives birth to sin, and sin when it is fully grown brings forth death"* (ESV).

Sin thrives on temptation, yet the only power temptation possesses is convincing us that somehow our lives will be better if we succumb to our indecencies. It's the man who thinks another woman will give him what he is lacking with his spouse. It's the drug addict who thinks they can quit anytime while they watch their world deteriorate from the inside out. It's chasing one dopamine spike after another, always expecting that the next choice will be what fulfills, but it never does.

Sin's progression is predictable but subtle. Deception, conception, then destruction. It's a pattern used by Satan since the beginning. We snidely belittle Eve for her lack of self-control, though we fall for the same trick just as often. She was deceived to believe she deserved more. She believed the lie that the apple would make her happy, and as much as we blame Satan for the temptation, he was playing on her internal desires. We are living in the aftermath of Satan's deception and Eve's capitulation.

No matter how much we would like to convince ourselves otherwise, sin never stays dormant. Its end goal is always destruction.

THE RUBBER BAND MAN

The pain shot through my hand and I recoiled as quickly as I could. I suppose it was my fault. I agreed to play the game. Wait, game? No, it wasn't a game. It was a tortuous battle of testosterone and I refused to lose. Now it was my turn to inflict the hurt. I took my rubber band and stretched it tightly between my fingers. After placing it on the back of my friend's hand, I pulled one side back as far as I could, then let it go with the fury of a thousand warriors. I'm convinced that some-one in Asia was awakened by the crack that reverberated through the atmosphere.

My friend realized two things very quickly. One, his rubber band may have been thicker and stronger, but it could not stretch as far, so it was ineffective for the game. And two, he could not sustain many more hits like what I had just unleashed or his hand might explode. I must admit, as a fourteen-year-old boy, I thought that would have been pretty cool. My friend conceded and I was the rubber band champion for the day.

I don't know why we thought it would be a good idea to snap each other's hands with rubber bands until one of us tapped out. I guess we were running out of things to do in between classes, and finishing homework early wasn't very alluring.

We never played that game again, but I learned a couple of valuable lessons. I learned a welt on a hand can last all day. I also learned the thicker and tougher the rubber band, the less effective it was. Conversely, if the rubber band was too thin, it would break when stretched. There was a happy medium when it came to rubber bands. It needed to be flexible yet also resistant to breaking when stretched to its capacity.

Humans aren't that different from rubber bands. The demands of change pull us in opposing directions. On one side exists the person we used to be. On the other side exists the person we want to become, the person God is calling us to become. We've existed in this tension since birth. There are days when we overcome the stress. Then there are days when we seem to buckle immediately at the slightest disruption. Each day we open our eyes to a sobering realization, that though the tension subsides on some days, it never truly leaves. I know this can sound quite ominous, but stay with me.

God loves you too much to let you stay the same. This is a good thing when the change is embraced. But what if it's something you don't want to change? If we're honest, we make choices each day that are not beneficial. For instance, I love donuts. I know donuts are bad for me. Aside from their deliciousness, they have no redeeming nutritional value, yet I still buy donuts. I know the consequences, but I still eat the occasional donut. I know in order to be the healthiest person I can be, I need to cut them out of my life no matter how good they taste.

How about you? What change has God been asking of you? Have you refused because you know it won't be easy? Or perhaps you expected the necessary change would stretch you beyond your breaking point? Do you need to change your diet? How about the people you allow to speak into your life? Do you feel better or worse after hanging around your group of friends? Is it your job? Your mindset?

You're at a crossroad. You can continue to drift, or you can choose to align yourself with God's best for your life.

The key to taking hold of God's best will be your malleability. The amount of stress an object can withstand before breaking is called its ultimate tensile strength. Some objects break quickly when pulled. Others are more malleable and can withstand a great deal more stress. We are human rubber bands, and our tensile strength is being tested daily. What is testing our spiritual tensile strength?

Sin and grace.

We exist in this strained space daily, and when the tension rises, we look for an escape. Sometimes we retreat to the person we used to be. That person may have been distraught, dysfunctional, and disappointing, but we know that person. As the saying goes, "Better the devil you know than the devil you don't." Your old self is misaligned but comfortable. People will tell you, "The past is in the past," but that's not quite true. Just because it no longer exists does not mean it cannot exist again. Sin relentlessly beckons us to dine at the deceivers table while the enemy arranges his ambush.

On one side is grace, purpose, and the voice of the Father inviting us to come. On the other side exists an alluring yet fractured future . Both are tugging with intensity at our destiny. Some days we slide to the left, sometimes to the right, but one thing is certain: we are always in the middle of this supernatural tug-of-war.

Sin will cause you to drift far beyond your ability to control. It begins gradually with masterful subtlety, but its desire is to own you. If you think your sin only affects you and you're not hurting anyone, it has already begun searing your conscience. Sin never remains isolated. It builds a demoralizing network within you, then explodes from you, spilling on those around you. You must address the sin issue in your life. It can't go unchecked if you desire health and wholeness.

DIFFERENT ENDINGS

When I was in elementary school, my favorite time of the year was when the book fair would visit. For a week they would set up shelves full of books and encourage us to guilt our parents out of their money for the sake of education.

Hands down, most fascinating books were the "choose your own adventure" books. Here, in my hands, rested the fate of the main characters. I had to choose their next path, and the wrong choice could end poorly. My heart would beat fast as I immersed myself in the magnitude of the responsibility. I was in control. I was the decision maker. Either they solved the mystery or the book came to an abrupt end. I know it doesn't seem like a big deal now, but when you are nine years old and have a vivid imagination, it is enthralling.

Much like the "choose your own adventure" books, we have two options that are continually before us. Choose life or choose death.

God sums this up so beautifully in Deuteronomy 30:19: "Today I have given you the choice between life and death, between blessings and curses. Now I call on heaven and earth to witness the choice you make. Oh, that you would choose life, so that you and your descendants might live!" (NLT).

Life and death, grace and sin, both pulling wildly at our soul, and due to our flawed nature, we are stuck in the middle. Every day we must make a conscious decision to lug ourselves toward life.

In 2 Corinthians 12:8–9, Paul says, "Three times I pleaded with the Lord about this, that it should leave me. But he said to me, 'My grace is sufficient for you, for my power is made perfect in weakness.' Therefore I will boast all the more gladly of my weaknesses, so that the power of Christ may rest upon me."

Humanity's default is to drift. The person we used to be is comfortable, even in dysfunction. We may agree, the person we used to be is not the person we should strive to become, but we are familiar with that person. We are not familiar with the person God is calling us to become, nor are we particularly comfortable with what it may take to get there.

Back to our saying "Better the devil you know than the devil you don't know." Frankly, I'd prefer no devil at all, but in the context of change and growth, we often feel more comfortable staying stagnant in familiarity than growing with discomfort.

Let's face it, if the person we used to be was that great, we wouldn't have needed to change, but don't look back. If it was a life without a relationship with Jesus, then it was a life worth leaving. But unfortunately, somewhere in that past life there is a veiled, comfortable feeling. We may not have been great, but we knew who we were.

The future presents a different set of circumstances. It's cloudy. We can't see that path as clearly as we can see our past. It's uncertain, and while it is cloaked with the promise of presence, power, and destiny, we hesitate to take one step. We immediately drift into every negative scenario. If history has told us anything, it's that destiny can be as detrimental as it can be fulfilling.

Depending on the trajectory your life has taken up to this point, the future will either be filled with fear, doubt, and insecurity, or excitement, hope, and purpose. I like what author Mike Connaway says in his book *Sabotage*:

> All thought patterns are set in stone, which is precisely why they call it a "mind-set." If our mind-set is wrong, then we will self-sabotage when it comes time to break out of our old thinking pattern and break into the new. In short, we are unable to reach our destiny because our mind would not allow it. Our mind wants order, thrives on order, and develops a pattern as quickly as possible to retain that order. If something new comes along —whether good or bad—that takes us out of our pattern, our mind revolts and tries to take us back to what is considered normal.

We cannot allow sin to be the normal thing in our lives. Sin should not make sense. It should not be comfortable. It should kick against everything Christ has done in you, through you, and for you.

The art of spiritual sabotage is part of our human make-up. We are forced to change the normal if we want to change our future. I think the power granted by our Savior is astounding in this measure. He gives us the ability to create a new story at any time, but this is not the best choice. The best choice is making sure our story is in alignment with His story. He beckons us to choose life and to follow His adventure story for our life.

Just like the books from my youth, every adventure has its profusion of pitfalls, but when God is steering your adventure, He never makes the wrong choice. Sure, you don't know what's on the other side of the chasm of forgiveness, faith step, or job transition, but you know if you are listening to the voice of the All-Knowing One, the end of your story will be beautiful, impactful, and memorable. It won't be safe, but you'll be secure. After all, the unknown isn't as scary if someone you love knows the way.

Sin promises the story will end well. It gives you a taste of satisfaction, prompting you to order the seven-course meal. It's not until you finish the last indulgent bite that you realize your appetite has not subsided. If anything, you are hungrier now than when you first began.

On the contrary, those who hunger and thirst for righteousness will be satisfied (Matthew 5:6). That Scripture could also be translated "those who hunger and thirst for righteousness will *have their fill.*" What a wonderful picture. It's not that you won't hunger, and it's not that you won't thirst, but when you do there is a spiritual buffet available. The food at this buffet isn't your traditional smorgasbord. No, this buffet is brimming with fine spiritual food, unattainable through your own efforts but given freely by His grace.

You don't have to let your momentary sin cause a permanent drift, but I'm not naive. Where you are may feel like a very dark place and you just can't seem to find the way back. This is the beauty of the God we serve. He doesn't need you to go back; He wants you to go forward. He doesn't hide the light for you to find. He brings the light to where you are and shows you the way.

Don't waste your time going back to who you used to be. It's time to discover the newly formed version of yourself (2 Corinthians 5:17).

WHAT GOOD MAY COME?

We know God rested on the seventh day, but you may not be aware of the majesty that occurred on the eighth day. God created coffee. You may not find it in the Scriptures, but it's true. Let's approach my theory with logic. He worked for seven days, took a nap, and when He woke up from His nap, He needed something to get going again, so He created the coffee bean. He knew humanity would need this organic fuel to accomplish such a great commission.

I'm joking, of course. Maybe.

If you are a coffee drinker, you're clearly walking in the anointing of the Father. As a coffee drinker, you may have experienced the unfortunate experience of drinking coffee grounds as the result of a malfunctioning coffee filter. As delicious as coffee is, a mouthful of gritty ground coffee beans is not pleasant at all. You need the coffee filter to remove the undesirable aspects of the bean so you can extract what you really want. If you fail to filter properly, your experience with coffee will be terrible.

Likewise, you will need to pass your sin through the filter of His grace so that what comes through is pure. Pastor Rick Warren declared something profound in his book *The Purpose Driven Life*: "If Paul had kept his experience of doubt and depression a secret, millions of people would never have benefited from it. Only shared experiences can help others. Aldous Huxley said, 'Experience is not what happens to you. It is what you do with what happens to you.' What will you do with what you've been through? Don't waste your pain; use it to help others."

There are people out there who will relate to your past sins. You just might be the light God is sending to show them what healing and wholeness could look like in their lives. The Enemy intended your sin to be your destruction, but God will use it as a compass, pointing them toward salvation. Sin will cause you to drift...

      every...

      single...

      time...

But the drift doesn't have to lead to your destruction.

"Jeremiah, say this to the people of Judah: 'This is what the Lord says: "When people fall down, don't they get up again? When they discover they're on the wrong road, don't they turn back?"'" (Jeremiah 8:4 NLT).

"The righteous falls seven times and rises again, but the wicked stumble in times of calamity" (Proverbs 24:16 ESV).

"The wicked are crushed by disaster, but the godly have a refuge when they die" (Proverbs 14:32).

"We are hunted down, but never abandoned by God. We get knocked down, but we are not destroyed" (2 Corinthians 4:9 NLT).

"Like a dog that returns to its vomit is a fool who repeats his folly" (Proverbs 26:11 NASB).

"It is good for me that I was afflicted, that I might learn your statutes" (Psalm 119:71 ESV).

SIX

....

THE ISOLATION DRIFT

In 1997 I stepped onto the Southeastern University campus in Lakeland, Florida, as a freshman, full of grand ideals and expectations. My parents were tearful as we said our goodbyes, but as an independent kid I couldn't wait to be on my own. I felt so grown up.

As I walked around campus, it seemed like everyone knew each other. Freshman, sophomores, juniors, and seniors mingled on the sidewalks and in the courtyards, all somehow connected. Everyone seemed connected. Everyone but me.

I still can't quite describe how I felt that first night as I lay in bed. I was always near friends and family. I had never felt lonely until that moment when my head hit the pillow. I could hear students' talking and laughter outside my window and wished I was with them. My best friend, Tad, and a few other friends would be arriving the next day, and that day couldn't come soon enough. In this moment of solitude I realized a disturbing truth: you can be surrounded by people yet feel very isolated and disconnected.

New York City has a population of over 8 million people, averaging over 27,000 people per square mile, yet people still feel alone. This deafening isolation causes a person to drift into a state of self-loathing, deprecation, and depression. We are designed to be social, so isolation, even for the introvert, is radically harmful. It's also very attractive. As much as we are created to be social beings, in times of pain we are drawn to aloneness.

My wife and I like to watch television shows together. We watch everything from cooking shows to car repair shows. One show we became particularly hooked on was called *Alone*. Ten contestants are dropped off in a remote part of the world with a small assortment of survival tools. They are required to hunt, fish, build a shelter, and find fresh water. They are confronted by bears, wolves, and other dangerous wildlife and they need to find a way to survive, all while recording themselves daily. At any time a contestant can tap out and a rescue team will come get them. Whoever can survive the longest wins $500,000.

We were initially drawn to the show because of the immediate threats the contestants faced, but we quickly realized this would not be what caused most of them to quit. The capable contestants found fresh water, built effective shelters, and began foraging for food. After they were safe, secure, and fed, the real battle began.

As the weeks passed, the overwhelming hurdle was not the cold, the hunger, or the diminished energy. It was the isolation. The contestants don't see anyone, hear anyone, or communicate with anyone. They must film themselves, feed themselves, and converse with themselves. Time and time again they would tap out, not because of malnutrition or physical threats, but because they couldn't take the isolation any longer. They would break down and cry, exert anger and frustration, and experience bouts of depression. Many experienced intense moments of clarity. They started to recognize what was important in their lives. The money no longer mattered. All they wanted to do was see their spouse, kids, friends, and family, and that connection became monumentally more important than winning half a million dollars.

Each person handled isolation differently, but each person felt the effects. Those who were a little more headstrong and were able to stay fed were most likely to win. The lure of the show is you never knew what was going to cause a person to drift to a place of no return. My wife and I were never very good at guessing who would win.

The contestants discovered the truth we tend to avoid. The isolation drift invites many deeply disturbing negative effects. Isolation has been linked to high blood pressure, inflammation, depression, sleep irregularity, susceptibility to viruses and illness, paranoia, and long-term mental disorders. People even tend to experience premature aging as a result of extended periods of solitude.

Despite all this data, when confronted with the challenges of life, many of us retreat into isolation. And this is exactly where Satan wants you. Isolation is a punishment, not a way of life, and the Enemy wants to punish you daily.

FAIL INTO EACH OTHER

"And let us consider how we may spur one another on toward love and good deeds, not giving up meeting together, as some are in the habit of doing, but encouraging one another—and all the more as you see the Day approaching" (Hebrews 10:24–25).

The author of Hebrews pulls no punches. He understands the natural tendency to withdraw into remoteness and spend the rest of our days practicing the art of the hermit. We conceal ourselves in our pain and find comfort in the snare of reclusion. We don't do this because we genuinely want to be alone. We do this because we don't feel we can truly be accepted in our imperfection. You may feel like a failure, but failure is a moment, not a person.

The Enemy seeks to deceive you, convincing you that solitude is the only option and healing only comes through seclusion, yet this is not what James 5:16 recounts: "Therefore, confess your sins to one another and pray for one another, that you may be healed. The prayer of a righteous person has great power as it is working" (ESV).

It's interesting how often the believer only quotes half of this verse. We love the power found in the prayers of the righteous, but we do not love that the context of this declaration is in the confession and collaboration of the body of Christ. God has nested our healing in relationships. He has not hidden it but provided a clear roadmap to the destination where wholeness is found. This may be a challenging concept for some of you because you've convinced yourself that you can honor God and live in isolation. The reality is the kingdom of God cannot be fully fulfilled in your life apart from other Christians.

I know. You may be thinking, *But I don't want to be around people! If they really knew what I've done, they wouldn't want to be around me either.* Yet God does not withdraw your value because of your mistake. There are still dreams and aspirations to which God is calling you, but none of your successes in the kingdom will exist outside the context of relationship.

Let's consider love. As elementary as this statement may be, you cannot learn to love apart from a relationship with someone else, and you likewise cannot receive love apart from somebody else. One of your most fundamental yearnings can only be satisfied in intimacy with another. This is the beauty of the Scriptures. We see a beautiful blend of personalities, backgrounds, and influence sitting at the table of redemption and sharing life together.

During biblical times, the societal caste system separated the wealthy and influential from the artisans and poor. A politician would never be caught dining with a carpenter. Jesus changed it all. Now people are eating together, laughing together, suffering together, with no regard to position or title.

This is what you are called to. A life of connection, encouragement, selflessness, and love. An isolated life removes you from all the benefits, exposes you to all of the abuse, and persuades you to find comfort in being forsaken. This is not God's call and it's not His intention. We are His family. The apostle Paul says it this way:

> *For as many as are led by the Spirit of God, these are sons of God. For you did not receive the spirit of bondage again to fear, but you received the Spirit of adoption by whom we cry out, "Abba, Father." The Spirit Himself bears witness with our spirit that we are children of God, and if children, then*

heirs—heirs of God and joint heirs with Christ, if indeed we
suffer with Him, that we may also be glorified together. (Ro-
mans 8:14–17 NKJV)

FINDING FAMILY

I used to meet with my friend Charles every Friday at seven
a.m. for breakfast. Our conversations were always exceptional, sway-
ing from discussions about church to technology and everything in
between. One of our conversations centered largely on our genera-
tional differences. He is sixteen years older than I am. We often see
the world and its inhabitants through different lenses, but both of us
desire to see things through God's eyes, as intimidating and overwhelming as that may be. In addition to our age gap is the disparity
in our cultural upbringing. He is a black man who was raised in West
Virginia. I am a white man who was raised twenty minutes outside of
Baltimore, Maryland. We look at the same world, but we interpret it
asymmetrically.

One particular morning we spoke about how our generations
view family. For many Gen Xers and millennials, family extends beyond blood and birth, and their attachment with these extended
connections can be just as deep. I embrace this ideology with heart
and soul, as I have one birth brother and an additional five men
whom I regularly introduce as my brothers.

While there is certainly no comparison to having a flesh-and-
blood family, with separation and distance comes the desire for intimacy. Millennials seek to create familial situations through their
friendships, especially if they have never experienced a cohesive

family. In situations where distance is prevalent, friends become family.

When we incorporate the spiritual implication of being sons and daughters of God, we find ourselves resolved to an unfamiliar dynamic. We are instantly surrounded by millions of people to which we are spiritually related, and if we have related poorly to our relatives in the past, we'll likely carry the same sensibility into God's kingdom. We aim to reproduce dysfunction in God's kingdom, not intentionally, yet willfully. When the dysfunction in the kingdom of God mirrors our own, we leave and we isolate. Turning our backs on our family becomes typical. We can spend all our emotional energy finding and cultivating a family environment, only to walk away from those very people who love us. When the going gets tough, we unfriend everyone and disappear from society.

Proverbs 24:10 renounces this mindset, stating, "If you falter in a time of trouble, how small is your strength!" This wasn't a question but an exclamation. A fact. It's an observational truth that reveals the correlation between the size of the fight in the dog versus the size of the dog in the fight. It's David versus Goliath. It's the hunter versus the hunted. It's left Twix versus right Twix. It's self versus family. Trouble can unite or divide. It can strengthen or it can cripple.

In a healthy and functional environment full of love and acceptance, to turn your back on family is spiritually and emotionally dysfunctional. It rejects the very intimacy Christ established through fathers and sons and mothers and daughters. At the same time, it celebrates division and isolation for the glory of self-prescribed remedies that are masked in the false identity of God's plan. Any plan that celebrates division is not of God; however, God does us a favor and instructs us how to deal with the divisive individual: "Warn *a divisive person once, and then warn them a second time. After that, have nothing to do with them. You may be sure that such people are warped and sinful; they are self-condemned" (Titus 3:10–11).*

It hurts when someone you love and consider family walks away from a relationship, a friendship, and/or the Lord. Very few things weigh so heavily on one's heart. This is why we do everything within our power to foster a sense of unity even in the midst of turmoil or conflict. Ephesians 4:1–6 encourages oneness and unity as part of our redemptive calling:

> *As a prisoner for the Lord, then, I urge you to live a life worthy of the calling you have received. Be completely humble and gentle; be patient, bearing with one another in love. Make every effort to keep the unity of the Spirit through the bond of peace. There is one body and one Spirit, just as you were called to one hope when you were called; one Lord, one faith, one baptism; one God and Father of all, who is over all and through all and in all.*

Sometimes we get tired and frustrated with family, and the frustration or fatigue fosters an us-versus-them mentality. It's not us versus them. It's simply us. We are all we have. Together. The kingdom of God is the kingdom of Together. It doesn't mean it will always be easy, but it will always be worth it.

FORGIVE THE OFFENSE

Harboring an offense is one of the quickest ways to send us into isolation. I have to laugh when I read John 21. Jesus calls out from the shoreline to the disciples who were struggling with their morning catch. Peter recognizes it is Jesus and flaunts his best Forest Gump impersonation. He jumps right off the boat and leaves the rest of the disciples to gather in the fish and row to shore. What would make him chase after Jesus so passionately that he would leave everything behind so quickly?

Denying the Messiah three times can sear the mind with painful memories. The moment Peter saw Jesus could have caused him to cower away, hide behind the other disciples, or bury himself under a tarp on the boat, but not Peter. Peter jumped off the boat and swam to Jesus. There was no waiting, no pausing, no helping with the fishing equipment. Forgiveness acts like that. Peter needed what Jesus longed to give. He aspired to restore Peter—to show him He had not lost faith in him despite Peter's transitory lapse of faith in Jesus.

Many people run from forgiveness. It's not that they don't need it. They just don't know they need it. Or maybe they don't want it, feel worthy of it, or wish to give it. Some offenses are forgiven quickly; some require more time. One thing is for certain: forgiveness carries its own pace. It craves quick reception but slow delivery. It is not forceful. Forgiveness carries a pace that is aligned with the soul but prolonged by the flesh.

Forgiveness is restorative and it heals the marred soul, but it is not easy to relinquish. The more serious the offense, the slower we desire forgiveness to move. We need time to feel sorrow, to feel hate, to cry, and to vent. Unfortunately, those feelings can contort, transforming momentary emotions into permanent perspective. If you're not careful, resistance to forgiveness will derail your mission and you'll be left holding your pride but little else. You may even wonder why God refuses to bless you to capacity.

When unforgiveness is your friend, isolation is your stomping ground. Those who are deeply offended and shelter unforgiveness view everyone as the enemy. Trust can't be given, and the only reprieve is relational segregation and spiritual confinement, yet the goal is not to forgive instantly. It's simply to follow the pace of forgiveness.

The pace of forgiveness is the pace of grace and mercy, both given abundantly by Christ. If you're in a place right now where you are finding it difficult to confront someone who has wronged you, to offer forgiveness, and to allow healing to take place, it's time to jump off the boat and swim toward Jesus. Living a life of unforgiveness is like riding a stationary bike and wondering why the landscape hasn't changed. It's not easy, but you can do it. You can claim a victory that the Enemy has desired to withhold from you. You are an overcomer, and you will find more freedom and strength in forgiveness than you ever thought possible.

I don't know what you've been through or what has been done to you, but I know the One who sits at the right hand of God, interceding for you. He has set before you the pace of forgiveness, and He asks for you to trust Him with the return. Your stride toward forgiveness will usually be slower than the beckoning of the Holy Spirit, but that doesn't mean you don't plod forward.

If Peter had not boldly swum toward Jesus, he may have lived his whole life with regret, bitterness, self-loathing, and a sense of emptiness, but Jesus restored him, gave him purpose, and set him on a mission. Peter became a pillar of the early church and a catalyst for global transformation.

Isolation is not your inheritance. God did not save you, heal you, and set you free to live in isolation. Find your tribe.

SEVEN

. . . .

THE GREATNESS DRIFT

James and John, the sons of Zebedee, came to him. "Teacher," they said, "we want you to do for us whatever we ask." "What do you want me to do for you?" he asked. They replied, "Let one of us sit at your right and the other at your left in your glory." "You don't know what you are asking," Jesus said. "Can you drink the cup I drink or be baptized with the baptism I am baptized with?" "We can," they answered. Jesus said to them, "You will drink the cup I drink and be baptized with the baptism I am baptized with, but to sit at my right or left is not for me to grant. These places belong to those for whom they have been prepared."

When the ten heard about this, they became indignant with James and John. Jesus called them together and said, "You know that those who are regarded as rulers of the Gentiles lord it over them, and their high officials exercise authority over them. Not so with you. Instead, whoever wants to become great among you must be your servant, and whoever wants to be first must be slave of all. For even the Son of Man did not come to be served, but to serve, and to give his life as a ransom for many." (Mark 10:35–44)

This story absolutely fascinates me. It speaks to the adolescence of the disciples. When we see their pictorial depictions throughout history, the disciples are presented as fully-grown men in their mid-thirties to early forties. Some historical artwork even paints them having white beards and balding. In reality, they were in their late-teens and early twenties.

Since rabbis were typically older than their students, and Jesus was thirty when He began His ministry, most estimate the disciples were between the ages of seventeen and twenty-five. Ranging from fisherman to tax collectors, they were old enough to engage in full-time work. They were young adults entrusted with spreading the most important message in the history of humankind.

When we look at Erik Ericson's stages of development, the basic conflict during this age range is isolation versus intimacy. What if the disciples would have had the emotional and mental development of today's college student? Can you imagine Peter pledging to a fraternity or Judas signing up for work-study in the accounting department? They craved intimacy and community. Jesus took these teenagers/young adults under his tutelage and trained them up in the way they should go.

When I think of myself in my twenties, I remember my arrogance, energy, and thirst for experience. I went off to college at eighteen years old and moved eight hundred miles away. I had a great upbringing, but it didn't prevent me from skipping class, staying out all night, and being morally irresponsible. I played numerous pranks on fellow students, served an in-school suspension the second semester of my freshman year, and struggled for years afterward to rebuild my GPA.

Granted, the disciples may have been more mature with their familial responsibilities, but when I read the Scriptures I can't help but picture them as the typical college student in search of identity and acceptance. So, when James and John (affectionately named "sons of thunder" by Jesus) present a request for position and greatness, I see it coming from teenagers who don't really know what they're asking.

I picture two young men with zeal, wrestling in the dirt, boisterous in their personalities. I picture my college friend Sean who occasionally blurted out wild and inappropriate things. I picture my best friend, Tad, who would run up and down the hallways of our dorm throwing M80s and pointing Saturn Missiles at our RA's door. I picture late-night Taco Bell runs and living on Ramen noodles. I picture some of the best times of my life. When I think of the disciples, I don't think of fully grown men. I think of who I was, and who I knew, in college.

James and John truly did not understand what they were asking. They could not comprehend the weight Jesus was carrying or the suffering He would endure. They did not understand the adversity greatness demands. It was an innocent, adolescent question from the start. As if Jesus was a genie, they asked, "Will you do for us whatever we ask?"

I imagine Jesus facetiously responding, "What do you want me to do for you?" If this were the twenty-first century, I imagine Jesus recording this conversation and posting the story on Instagram with the hashtags #thesekidsdontknow #adulting #millennials #entitled.

They wanted greatness by appointment. They wanted the crown of position, not the towel of servanthood. Jesus, as He did time and time again, realigned their mindset. Ruling is overrated. Serving is the new ruling. True greatness isn't found in our ability to administer. It's found in our willingness to consider others better than ourselves (Philippians 2:3) and serve with no regard for recompense.

It's frustrating to watch Christian leaders forget this significant lesson. If you're not careful, you'll allow your ambition for greatness to drive you to rule over others when you should reign on your knees.

Our prideful nature desires acknowledgement, respect, and admiration. We want to feel important, be important, and influence others to our whims. It's anarchy, a non-recognition of authority. We want to call the shots, not wash the feet of those who do. Celebrity ministers demand AAA 5 Diamond lodging, expensive meals, and high honorariums to communicate the gospel with the grace gifts they did not earn and the anointing they cannot manipulate.

I greatly respect the apostle Paul because while he raised support from churches, it was for the sole purpose of spreading the gospel. He suffered greatly for the cause of Christ, and he was worthy of the support given to him by the New Testament churches. Paul did not build palatial estates and drive Bentleys. I suppose I struggle with those who use the gospel to build their wealth portfolio. Do I believe wealth is bad? Absolutely not. There were numerous people in the Bible who were honored by God in this way. The difference? The wealth was granted, not requested.

I know, there are many nuances to this conversation. The laborer is worthy of his reward (1 Timothy 5:18; Matthew 10:10; Luke 10:7). There is clearly a precedent set to honor those who are obedient in their calling. There is also the conversation of spiritual gifts and spiritual fruit. Some people have more natural grace gifts than others. Some preachers can sing better than most worship leaders, preach better than most professional orators, write better than most authors, and lead better than most gurus. They are five-talent individuals and their unique abilities propel them to higher platforms. But was the platform their ambition, or did they simply strive to turn their five talents into ten? I would argue, more often than not, their obedience made way for their greatness. They are able to turn five talents into ten, so you pay them accordingly. You would not give the same reward to the person who did not manage one talent well.

Perhaps this is a soapbox, a brief digression, but I refuse to believe greatness is established through social media followers and material gain. In fact, greatness is not granted by humankind at all. As a subject in the kingdom of God, only the King can invite us to the table. Promotion comes from the Lord. The Lord gives and the Lord takes away (Job 1:21). The Lord sees the heart, and every motive is laid bare before Him (Matthew 12:25; Jeremiah 20:12; Matthew 22:18; Luke 16:15; Acts 15:8).

It's not wrong to have nice things, but remember, those things you strive so valiantly to attain will one day end up in the trash. People are the only thing of eternal value worth fighting for.

When serving is your number one priority, material gain becomes less attractive. All you care about is how to serve more. If the Lord promotes you, He will keep you, as you have likely already shown yourself faithful with very little (Luke 16:10), but beware. Just because you were faithful with little doesn't mean you'll be faithful with much. David didn't make his mistakes as a shepherd; he made them as a king.

GRASS AND GLORY

It is unlikely that anyone has ever referred to you as being grass, and it is equally unlikely that you would receive it well if it did in fact happen. We are not to be compared to something lacking the natural God-given dynamic attributes of humanity. We mow grass; it's not our identity.

Then again, God has a peculiar way of using imagery, metaphor, and simile in the Scriptures to illuminate our understanding as well as douse us with a hefty load of perspective. Saint Peter, the apostle, connects our humanity with our accomplishments, our "grass and our glory" (1 Peter 1:24–25). We are grass, and our glory is like the flowers of the field.

It paints a pretty picture, doesn't it? Are you picturing a beautiful field of lush green grass with random yellow flowers peppered throughout? Of course, the sky in your imagination is bluer than blue, at least if our minds are visiting the same field.

It isn't the celebration of our humanity or the glory of our accomplishments that draw the focus of these verses. It's not the buildings we build, the books we write, or the relationships we've cultivated. It isn't the inventions we've dreamed or the songs we've written that attract the praise in this instance. In fact, the only praise presented is in opposition of what we would define as success.

Our humanity is like grass, our glory is like the flowers of the field, and then comes the kicker: grass withers and flowers fall.

It screams of fragility and finality. In no place does it call into account our desired legacy or imprint on humanity. These are glories we would chase, and some rather fervently. I am as guilty as all. I have a recurring thought, a haunting vision, a self-glorifying desire to be *remembered*. I marvel at spiritual giants such as A. W. Tozer and C. S. Lewis and Dietrich Bonhoeffer who, not desiring sustained glory but sustaining faith, are honored more now than when they were alive.

God chooses to exalt in this measure. It is the individuals who offered themselves to the service of our Lord, the ones who were "poured out like a drink offering" (Philippians 2:17) on sacrifice and service, who have positioned themselves to receive, however God is the source.

One of my mentors, Dr. Rhoden, once explained, "The Lord is not always fair, but He *is* always just." We prefer preferential treatment. We desire to receive the same blessing as the most blessed individual, but not everyone is a ten-talent individual (Matthew 25:14–30). We did not get to craft ourselves or select our capacity or spiritual gifts. Our essence is not customizable. There is only one version of you, and it is the right version—the just version—but, in our eyes, not always the fair version.

In *The Signature of Jesus*, Brennan Manning notes, "The Holy Spirit is the bearer of gifts and these gifts are sometimes lavished in peculiar places. God bestows his grace abundantly but unevenly. He offers no explanation why some are called to radical discipleship and others are not." We may not understand why God chooses to exalt some and allow others to simply rejoice in His favor and invitation to mercy. We may desire kingdom impact and a legacy that will follow us after we have departed into the sunset. The reality is only "the word of the Lord endures forever" (1 Peter 1:25).

Something tells me when we are standing in the presence of our King, we will pay little mind to our past "glory," as it has likely begun its descent toward withering and falling. We will become reflective and entranced with the heart-piercing question, *What did I do that was worth Christ dying for?*

If glory is not the answer and our longevity is not promised, how are we to attain greatness for God? How are we to intentionally avoid elevating our own glory while simultaneously pursuing a call that may launch us into a place of noticeability?

One word.

One word aligns our character, controls our substance, and places us in a position of honor. God needs only one word to describe the way we are to serve him. Only one word will unlock the mysteries of heaven. This word drives every ounce of the human's connection to Him. It's one of those words that, when repeated incessantly, begins to sound like not much of a word at all. It certainly offers itself as a meaningless sound more so than a description of earth's inheritor.

The word is *meekness.*

John A. Redhead noted that it is so easy to mistake one of the signs of a thing for the thing itself. For instance, a star gives light, and so does a lantern, but a lantern is not a star. It is all too easy to associate meekness with weakness. We see restraint and we confuse it with inability. We see timing and we confuse it with passivity. It's important to understand why Jesus proclaimed that the meek would inherit the earth (Matthew 5:5), but to do that we must first begin by clearing up the sullied name meekness has attained.

Aristotle describes meekness as the golden mean between extreme anger and extreme angerlessness. It is the great in between, but when we look at meekness, we find it truly has nothing to do with weakness and much more to do with controlled strength. John Redhead described it best when he said, "The meek man is the man who is always angry at the right time and never angry at the wrong time."

We can best relay the idea of meekness to animals. A horse bucks when it does not want to be ridden. It may be because the saddle is uncomfortable or because it had a bad experience being ridden in the past. It may be because the horse has too much energy; a horse penned up for too long may buck upon release.

Does a horse's giving permission to the rider to guide it make the horse any less powerful? Certainly not! Meekness is a will, much like a wild horse, that has been tamed and submitted.

You may have always accepted the posture of strength, of authority, of vocal abrasion to enact your will. Shouting may have been excused as you rode the myth of greatness through forceful coercion. If so, you couldn't be further from the message of Jesus. I'm not saying there shouldn't be an unbridled fire burning inside of you. I would prefer that there were. It's even okay to be angry. Jesus displayed moments of wrath that are talked about in movies and written about in plays, but He was simultaneously meek. The meek man is the man who is always angry at the right time and never angry at the wrong time.

The meek have inherited, and will continue to inherit, the earth. Those who preached the message of love, who preached the message of Jesus, have multiplied over the centuries, and earthly kingdoms have come and gone.

Force will always encounter a greater force. No boxing champion holds his title forever. No building stands for eternity. No army prevails forever and no human is invincible, but love will never be conquered. Love is brash enough to outlast any menacing desire and kind enough to salve any injured emotional wound. Love has a way of being violent and unapologetic but never in an offensive way. The strong would see no need for such a tool. It is their desire to impose their will, not follow the will of the Lord.

If you seek to impose your will upon life, you will resent any interference. When you go broke or go blind and everything goes berserk, your castle in the sand will be dashed to pieces by one little wave of misfortune.

But isn't *strength* a more attractive word than *meekness*? Meekness is not innately desirable. Meek is not a part of our nature. Strength, on the other hand, is admired. Strength is respected. Acts of strength are envied. We have little respect for the man or woman who is frequently abused or taken advantage of due to their lack of strength.

It is the strong that raise the banners of success while the meek clean up the confetti.

We idolize the heroics of King Leonidas and his brave battle at Thermopylae. "Here is a man of strength!" we laud as we purchase the movie ticket eager to see this demonstration of strength so that we may strive to be just as strong.

What advantage exists within meekness that can't be magnified with the pure force of strength? Who would choose to deny themselves strength's prowess in exchange for something as insignificant as meekness?

Jesus would.

Perhaps that is why this is so confusing—so upside down. Why would the all-powerful God desire we be meek? Clearly there are none more powerful than someone who is all-powerful. Surely those who could never *be* Him do not threaten him. Why meekness?

Would not a loyal army of the powerful and strong accomplish far more in far less time than the meek? Would you not prefer an army cloned from Leonidas in lieu of an army of the scared and feeble? In battle, would we not side with the most powerful instead of the most humble?

Maybe in our kingdom, but we are redeemed by the power of the cross. We are no longer bound to, or obligated to follow, the rules of *our* kingdom. Any strength expressed in *our* kingdom is pseudo-strength. We may be strong in our kingdom, but our greatest strength in God's kingdom is still weakness. Ironically, meekness in God's kingdom propels us to great strength.

STRENGTH'S SECRET

I should note that strength does in fact have a secret. It is a secret only revealed to us when we surrender all we have to discover it. We surrender our families, friends, and possibly even our future to learn this secret. We turn our backs on those who care for us, and we pretend to care for those who may grant us access to strength's secret.

On this road to the unveiling of strength's secret, we encounter many wonderful things. We may achieve financial wealth. We may win awards and recognition, and people may cheer our name. Our faces may grace the cover of nationally read magazines, our schedules will yield no white space, and we may have to silence our phones as cable news programs and talk shows beg for our attention. *Our* attention.

Who, with their mind correct, would not desire to achieve strength?

Ah, but then the secret is revealed. After all has been accomplished and we finally feel *strong*, the ever-evasive enigma becomes known, and we are forced to encounter a feeling we never expected.

Weakness.

We realize that no matter how hard we try to be strong, we cannot control the finale of our life. No matter how much strength we amass, we are incapable of sustaining our very breath. God knows strength is not longstanding. Strength distracts from the advancement of *His* kingdom. Strength would bring temporary pleasure but would sacrifice eternal impact. Strength is nothing more than withering grass and falling flowers. But the word of the Lord... love... endures forever.

In God's greatest move of establishing an upside-down kingdom, He immediately removes the very thing that one would expect necessary to rule a kingdom. He esteems the meek and in doing so quenches our insatiable desire for strength. *Our* kingdom requires strength, but His requires meekness.

God's kingdom is reliant on His strength. His limitless strength extends beyond our existence. When we release our last breath, His strength resumes. Realizing that we can never really achieve strength releases our need of it. When the option of strength is removed, we are left with God's perfect intention: meekness.

God quickly recognizes those who choose meekness. King David had every right to walk in strength. He had been meek early, but once he transcended the common person, he began to embrace the idea of *strength over meekness*. He demonstrated his grip on strength by releasing his grip on God. He took hold of his strength and began to act in ways that would cause others to acknowledge him as strong. He lost sight of the meek only to regain perspective after an encounter with an old friend.

At David's moment of vulnerability, it was not the power, prestige, or position that gave him comfort. His prayer, his cry, his plea was that God would not remove His presence.

In God's kingdom, strength is a weakness. Human strength in our kingdom limits godly strength and advancement in His kingdom.

What about the part about inheriting the earth? Doesn't it always seem that the assertive and malicious gain while the meek are left wondering how strength and glory slipped through their fingers? Whenever we speak of an "inheritance," we tend to think of something grandiose. We think about the will that entitles us to millions of our predecessors' money. We dream about the mansion. We dream about the old sports car that we'd now be able to claim as our own.

Why do the meek deserve an inheritance? Wouldn't it seem logical that the assertive would be best suited for managing the weight of the world? Should we not assume the alpha-male, type-A personality, be the only one trusted with such a valuable and extensive task?

However gracious meekness may appear, do not be mistaken. Meekness is supported by incomparable power.

Meek may rhyme with *weak*, but they most certainly are not synonymous. To be meek is not to be void of strength. To be meek is to understand the source of the strength and offer the essence of our being to that source, including our emotions, ambitions, and intellect.

Meekness is surrendering personal greatness and personal ambition in response to the easy and light calling of Jesus. The meek inherit the earth because they are completely surrendered to God and not the ambition of greatness. If God should choose to exalt, it would not be denied, and if God would choose to withhold, it would be accepted graciously. The exaltation of *self* requires the strength of *self*, and any failed attempts will be openly attributed to *self*.

On the other hand, exaltation by God allows the infinite power of God to be released liberally. The reception of such power elicits the recognition of God's identity and enlightens the path where this divine identity is captured in our surrender.

It is in this surrender, this infinite resignation, that we find our inheritance. It is impossible to forcibly inherit, so any action on our behalf to acquire the earth would be futile, as it was never ours to acquire. It is ours to receive, not take, but His to give. This is where Jesus' words evolve from allegory to significance.

The strong gain but they do not acquire. They take but they do not receive. The earth belongs to those who would accept it from its owner.

One last thought, this one concerning leadership. It is impossible for the evidence of strength to coexist with the nature of meekness. Leaders will often applaud the meek as long as the meek submit to their desires. When the meek rise up, and rightfully so, a leader who is leading from their strength will always attempt to grasp the upper hand. They will control the relationship, the conversation, and the result. They will squash the meek with their power, and in doing so will forfeit the kingdom God has created for them.

Those leading from their own strength will *never* be successful in God's kingdom. It is far too upside down for that.

EIGHT

THE FULFILLMENT DRIFT

"Wouldn't you want your daughter to be happy?" asked the single young pastor sitting in my office.

I paused for a moment, then replied, "No."

He gazed at me, stunned and speechless.

I let the tension linger because I wanted him to hear my reasoning. "When you have kids, you'll quickly realize their inability to discern what is good and what is harmful. The harmful things can be disguised as wonderful in moderation but detrimental in excess. My daughter would eat candy for breakfast, lunch, and dinner, and that would make her happy, but as a parent I understand the harm it would cause, so I have to say no to her request to eat gummy bears for dinner and make sure she eats something more sensible, like grilled chicken and broccoli. Your kids will not always know what is best for them, and you will have to be okay with their unhappiness if it supports their greater well-being."

He dropped his head and his eyes teared up. He was struggling both relationally and professionally. He was beginning to question his path and God's fathering ability. He genuinely thought that following Jesus would mean a life free from struggle. Unfortunately, our obedience to the Father does not preclude others from their obedience to the flesh. Just because we are in His will doesn't mean others aren't carving out a separate path of unrighteousness. This pastor was hurting, and he wanted to be happy, but what he needed was a new framework to process his suffering. He was obedient yet felt punished.

"Listen, we live in a time when followers of Jesus pursue happiness over obedience," I went on. "If the season, action, or responsibility does not incite continuous happiness, they feel they missed the mark. Yet, I doubt the apostle Paul was 'happy' when he was beaten, stoned, shipwrecked, mocked, and imprisoned. I doubt Jesus was 'happy' when He was scourged and nailed to a cross. Their fulfillment was not found in their circumstance, yet they were fulfilled. Somehow, supernaturally, fulfilling the mission of the King brings great fulfillment in us. I suppose it makes sense when we understand God's composition. There is nothing we can add to God to make Him greater, and there is nothing we can withhold from God to reduce His greatness. He is perfection, and perfection cannot be improved upon (Matthew 5:48), therefore, whenever we operate in His perfect plan, the grace of fulfillment will always flow down. We are fulfilled because it was God's intention for us to feel such a thing."

We make great strides toward drifting when we look outside of God for our fulfillment. When we place our hope in the carnal instead of the eternal, hope shifts within us. In fact, many who have placed hope in carnal things are not only let down, beat down, and torn down. No, they experience a tragedy that claims lives every day.

Hopelessness.

Some may even say they have "lost hope," but I disagree. You can never lose hope because hope is foundational to the human experience. You haven't lost hope; you've simply misplaced it. The problem is, misplacing hope can be worse than losing it altogether. Hope cannot be extinguished, and this misplaced truth is what magnifies the anguish. We would miss hope if it were lost, but we would adapt and move on. However, hope is eternal. Even after it's been misplaced, it shows up again the next day, beckoning us to be better stewards, as hope can be quite fragile.

We place hope in people and are abandoned (I'm looking at you, Judas). We place hope in material things only to see them deteriorate and break (Matthew 6:19). We put hope in money, but it is intentionally insatiable (Ecclesiastes 5:10). We chase what we don't have, thinking it to be the missing piece to our joy and fulfillment. We are very quick to misplace our hope. It's fascinating to think how we avoid depositing our hope in the One who does not benefit from our hope.

Hope was masterfully crafted into our DNA along with the ability to create, marking our similarity to the Father. We create beautiful symphonies, build majestic buildings, and write emotionally moving songs out of nothing. It didn't exist until we thought of it, formed it, and nurtured it, and it now exists in mature form.

God has given you the ability to use many things but none greater than His Spirit. Money is a tool, relationships are an asset, and work brings provision, but none of those things can perfectly cradle our hope free from harm.

If you want happiness, joy, and fulfillment, you must begin with reinvesting your hope in the eternal. Perhaps we can all declare like David:

We put our hope in the Lord.
He is our help and our shield.
In him our hearts rejoice,
for we trust in his holy name.
Let your unfailing love surround us, Lord,
for our hope is in you alone. (Psalm 33:20–22 NLT)

This realization did not cease with David. The apostle Paul had a similar revelation when he declared he had found the secret of contentment: he could do all things through Christ who strengthened him (Philippians 4:12–13).

Let me give you a tip as you traverse through life's peaks and valleys. Chase obedience over fulfillment. Fulfillment can be emotionally contingent and wildly unpredictable. What fulfills one day may bring misery the next. Don't focus on fulfillment; focus on obedience. Obedience is rooted in faith and is propelled by trust. Trusting in the One who stands outside of time and knows the beginning from the end is a wise decision. We try to be the adult in our relationship with God, but in reality, we are the kid demanding ice cream for dinner and then throwing a temper tantrum when we don't get our way. If only we realized our obedience, while not tasty at the time, would lead to greater spiritual health and vitality.

SOLOMON WAS WRONG

Solomon was wise but not perfect, so when I read the book of Ecclesiastes, perhaps I read it a little different than most. While some read and see profound revelation as to the meaninglessness of life, I see a bitter and bored man who had drifted. In fact, there is an entire chapter devoted to Solomon's errors (1 Kings 11).

I believe many make the mistake of reading Ecclesiastes as the musings of an infallible man because he was the "wisest man who ever lived," yet He disobeyed God, committed idolatry, rebelled against God's Word, and hardened his heart to the things of God. I don't say this to belittle his accomplishments but to help you understand that his pensiveness may have been flawed. Is everything really meaningless? When I read the Scriptures, I am embraced by the announcement that we are His workmanship, we are chosen, we are given a great commission. Since when did God create anything without intention?

God's creation and purposes have never been meaningless. What we create, on the other hand, may be quite meaningless if it is not connected to the purpose of the Father. Everything God created was for **His** glory and pleasure (Revelation 4:11). Our creations tend to be for **our** glory and pleasure.

Solomon was right, but not in the way he intended. Many things are meaningless, but it's not because of their nature. It's because of their motive. Work is great, unless you disobey the commands of the Lord, neglect your family, and use it to gain material wealth to fill an un-fillable void. Friends are essential (Proverbs 27:17) but are often unpredictable and inconsistent. Money can advance the kingdom or it can magnify our internal defects. This is the carnal approach to fulfillment, declaring the sense fulfillment is primary. It promotes the idea wherein everything we do ought to bring fulfillment, and if fulfillment were to wane, we must abandon everything to find it once again. If your spouse no longer fulfills, divorce them. If your job no longer fulfills, quit. If your friends no longer fulfill, cut them out. If your employees no longer fulfill, write them off, fire them, or make their lives miserable until they hand in their resignation. If your pursuit of a higher education no longer fulfills, change your major.

The biblical approach to fulfillment is quite the opposite. Fulfillment is not in achieving our wants, wishes, and desires. It is anchored in obedience, not accomplishment. Biblical fulfillment is never cloaked in comparison. Fulfillment will ultimately come when we place our trust in God, as He works all things for the good of those who love Him and are called according to his purposes (Romans 8:28).

Every decision you make must be anchored in this unwavering revelation; there is never a time when God is not working toward what is best for you. God is refining the parts you'd least like to surrender.

One of the Scriptures I loathe is 1 Peter 5:10, which says, "And the God of all grace, who called you to his eternal glory in Christ, after you have suffered a little while, will himself restore you and make you strong, firm, and steadfast." There is a promise of restoration, but there is also a certainty of suffering. There is no joy in suffering, but you can withstand the storm when you understand a season is not a sentence. It's not permanent. The fulfillment is in the restoration, but restoration is not possible without deconstruction.

I love watching automobile restoration shows. I could sit and watch them for hours. It's the "before and after" that is so addicting. The same formula is found in fitness, weight loss, and real estate shows. There is what used to be, glimpses of what could be, and the final revealing of what has become. When the master mechanics choose to restore a vehicle, they often do a "frame-off" restoration. The body is removed from the car and the frame is thoroughly inspected. It is repaired, refreshed, and repainted, ensuring the structural integrity for the changes to come. It doesn't make much sense to fix the body if the frame is rusting, twisted, or cracked. The car may still look nice, but it may not last long, not to mention the safety risks attached to a deteriorated frame. The fulfillment will only be partial. You'll love the look but won't have faith in the integrity of the car.

When God created us, He did so in His image (Genesis 1:27). He established a beautiful, uncompromised frame and filled it with His Spirit. Sin corrupted our fragile structure to the point it can no longer be repaired, so God instead creates something completely new (2 Corinthians 5:17). Unfortunately, instead of walking in our newness, we focus our strength on repairing the former frame. Instead of finding fulfillment in the new, we look to repair the old. We want to be who we were but with different results.

Impatience will inevitably surface on your journey toward fulfillment. You may need to remind yourself daily that the tension is temporary and all value must be placed on each step of obedience.

There is an expectation in Scripture that life will be challenging (James 1:2-4; John 16:33; Romans 12:2; Psalm 55:22; Romans 5:3–5). Can you imagine if Jesus had abandoned His mission? Instead of praying the Father's will be done (Luke 22:42), what if He exclaimed, "If you don't take this cup from me, I quit!"

Did Jesus have moments where He thought to Himself, *This isn't fulfilling at all*? Jesus clearly expressed frustration, anger, and impatience, so there must have been moments when the human frame waged war against the Spirit man. Jesus didn't need to be made new since He was never corrupted by sin, yet one could argue that the Enemy was after the fruit of the Spirit within Him. How often have you sinned out of frustration? Anger? Apathy? Emotions are powerful things, and if we convince ourselves fulfillment is found in the emotional peaks alone, we won't be able to withstand the valleys of obedience.

If we're honest, we admire those who traverse through great adversity only to accomplish the impossible. We esteem those who wear their wounds well. If we're honest, we desire similar accomplishments without the lashings that provide them. We want the cup but not the cross.

Safety is overrated. As much as I want my daughter to be safe and only experience unimaginable success, I also understand I have little control over these things. Like many parents, fear can grip my heart when I think of this world's perversions. I pray protection over my family constantly. While I don't want them to experience pain, as a father my responsibility is to prepare them as best I can for the inevitable. Why would our heavenly Father behave differently?

Fall in love with the process toward fulfillment and you may find yourself echoing the apostle Paul's revelation: "I have learned the secret for contentment."

PART TWO

BACK ON COURSE

Being aware of your fear is smart. Overcoming is the mark of a successful person.
– Seth Godin

Above all the grace and the gifts that Christ gives to His beloved, is that of overcoming self.
– Francis of Assisi

In part one we focused on identifying the various drift catalysts. In part two, I will provide some practical steps to prevent drifting in the future. To avoid drifting you must live with great intention. Every season offers opportunity. Claim yours.

NINE

....

FEEL

Men tend to prefer feeling numb over being emotive; however, when God created man, he did not withhold any emotions. We feel the wide range but have allowed cultural expectations to mute those feelings deemed less "manly," yet emotions are core to our humanity. Men feel passion, apathy, fear, hate, frustration, sadness, and joy, but in a time of rampant fatherlessness, proper emotions are no longer modeled. Instead we are immersed in a pseudo-masculine environment shaped by the shows we watch and the movies we adore.

Yet when I read the Scriptures, I see leader after leader express the gamut of emotional manifestation unapologetically. We experience critical circumstances that are *supposed* to leave us in a puddle of brokenness. Those who are unable to feel are labeled sociopaths.

If you are drifting, you'll eventually come to a moment of remarkable clarity. Past decisions will haunt you and aim to define you, and you'll find yourself suddenly overwhelmed. You'll look in the mirror, hate what you see and not know how you became that person, and long to go back a day, a week, or a year and talk some sense into your past self—but you can't. This adds to the hopeless feeling in your gut, and suddenly you hear the voice of the Enemy louder than any other time in your life: "You're a failure. God doesn't love you. Your family will never forgive this. You'll never get over this. This is who you are. Just give up."

Cue breakdown.

In order to get back on course, you must find a safe place to express externally your internal conflicts. It means presenting ourselves to the Lord and allowing the Holy Spirit to both convict and heal, comfort and correct. When sin has taken root, you quickly become desensitized to the ramifications of your decisions. The more frequently you engage in the wrong action, the more hardened your heart becomes. The Enemy doesn't want you to feel the weight of your drifting. He will attempt to convince you it's not that bad and everyone else is overreacting. He wants indifference. He wants you to be numb because he understands the Lord is attracted to a broken spirit and repentant heart as a moth is to the flame (Psalm 51:17). If Satan destroys your intimacy, he can isolate you from the heart of the Father.

So what does "feeling" look like?

The human brain will naturally find ways to cope with trauma, loss, and pain. A friend of mine lost his mother in a car accident when he was in his late twenties. His father was a successful pastor of an incredible church, and his mom had a leadership and teaching anointing on her life. Whenever she taught a class or a group, hundreds of women would show.

When my friend got the phone call that his mother had been in an accident and died from her injuries, he struggled to feel. He had a mission trip to lead, youth camps to lead, and ministry to facilitate. He filled every second of every day with activity and never processed his pain.

One day, as he was driving, he received a call from a mentor. The mentor simply asked him how he was doing processing the loss of his mom. In that moment he realized he had never actually grieved her passing. It wasn't that she was unimportant, quite the opposite. Suddenly, every emotion came bubbling to the surface and he pulled his car onto the shoulder of the road and wept. That was the beginning of his healing.

As you make your way back on course, allow yourself to feel the ramifications of drifting. Allow yourself to feel the pain of those you've hurt. The lives you've seemingly ruined. The loss of vision and purpose. The ministry position you no longer hold because of a moral failure. The spouse who left because you neglected them. The success you allowed to take priority. The indifference from disappointment and unmet expectations. The emotional and physical exhaustion that taints every thought with bitterness and loathing.

If you refuse to admit there is an open wound, you'll never allow God to be your Healer. Lean in, not out. Find your tears again and allow the presence of God to wash over you. Allow Him to put you back together and place your feet on solid ground. He loves you and is ready for you to get back on course.

Please don't misunderstand the purpose of this chapter. It's not to make you feel worse about your decisions. It's about exchanging the ashes of your torched life for a garment of praise. It's giving the Lord your hardened heart and waking up to find one of flesh in its place.

Give it time. For some of you, everything will change in an instant. For others, it will be after years of counseling, searching, and rebuilding yourself into the person God intended from creation. Be patient. You will get there.

THICK SKIN, TENDER HEART: A LEADERSHIP CONVERSATION

The statement resonated so deeply within me. It was a recent social media post from a friend. As I read, I couldn't help but feel my inner man jump with affirmation. Almost flippantly within the context of a longer post, he said, "We don't have to allow sin against us to produce sin within us." I felt like shouting, "Preach!"

Isn't this one of the greatest challenges when leading others? We internalize strife and erect great relational walls so that we never have to experience pain or rejection. Unchecked, we have a propensity to equate thick skin with a hardened heart. In fact, it is often the most offensive and demeaning person who lauds that others should develop this thick skin. Those unapologetic few simply want to be able to speak without reserve, restraint, or filter, with no negative ramifications. It. Just. Won't. Happen.

If life and death are truly in the tongue, then we are not responsible only for what we say. We are also responsible for the littered, bloody bodies left behind our words. It's not just the spoken word, but those unspoken that can also lead to a hardened heart. The disgusted glance, the roll of the eyes, and deliberate avoidance mar the hapless souls who cross the path of the insecure leader.

They exhort, "Develop thicker skin. Don't let anything hurt you or offend you."

I reply, "Develop the fruit of the Spirit. You can't love from a distance."

So which statement is right?

There is a great deal of validity to developing thick skin, but the purpose of thick skin is not so that we can say or do as we please, or so that we no longer have to feel. We must develop thick skin to prevent untruths from penetrating the tender heart. The problem with most leaders is that they allow insecurities to keep their skin thin and expose their heart to suffering. In doing so they only have one course of action. Harden the heart. Don't let anyone in, refuse to trust, and push others down instead of building them up. Highlight their glaring mistakes instead of helping them over-come and excel. It's the soul tattoo of the insecure leader. When they talk to you about others, they frequently mention those people's shortcomings. Rest assured, they will do the same to you. Your shortcomings will also become their tagline.

The insecure leader does not always realize what they are doing. They may be 100 percent accurate and 1,000 percent wrong. The insecure leader uses fear, intimidation, and manipulation to get the results they are after. The insecure leader will reduce others if it makes them look wiser or stronger.

The difference between the insecure leader and the secure leader could not be more noticeable. The secure leader will always lead people to think the best of their co-workers and co-laborers, not plant seeds of doubt as to their ineffectiveness. They will highlight their strengths and cover their weaknesses. They will praise them in public and in private. They will speak life. The environment of the secure leader is safe. Not easy, but safe (much like our relationship with Father God). The secure leader finds joy when those they lead surpass them in accomplishment. They never diminish or taint the successes of others with snide remarks or devaluing quips.

While this should be magnified in the life of the spiritual leader, the spiritual leader also contends with the spiritual realm. After all, the Enemy does not waste bullets on dead soldiers. If you're an effective leader but also an unbeliever, he may very well leave you to your own devices. The spiritual leader is warring for eternal destinies, so their temptations are that much greater.

We all know a pastor or spiritual leader who has made the mistake of thinking they could possess thin skin *and* a softened heart, only to be wounded beyond repair. They become jaded toward people, toward vision, and toward their own calling. Doubt, regret, and judgment become their native tongue, and they relive the same wounds time and again, which feeds into their insecurity.

You may also know a leader who has thick skin and a hardened heart. The challenge with this leader is they may actually be quite successful. Their thick skin protects their heart from untruths and allows them to hear the voice of God. This may lead you to ask, "If thick skin protects the heart, how then did their heart become hard?"

Great question. The answer is most often found in the past. Their heart hardened because of a past wounding at a time when they had thin skin. They thickened their skin but never dealt with the wounded heart. These are the most vexing of all leaders. They are now un-offended but also untouchable, isolated, and withdrawn from relationships. They don't trust but they don't distrust either. They can be open and sincere one moment, stubborn and uncaring the next. They are at conflict within themselves. They realize the need for thick skin, but they don't know what to do with the heart. It hurts too much, takes too much time, and they have better things to do than revisit the past to reclaim their tenderness.

God's promise to the people of Israel who had hardened their hearts and served idols becomes prophetic to today's leader: "And I will give you a new heart, and I will put a new spirit in you. I will take out your stony, stubborn heart and give you a tender, responsive heart" (Ezekiel 36:26 NLT).

The benefits of having thick skin and a tender heart are numerous:

* Thick skin will help you survive the critics, and the tender heart will lead you to pray for and bless them.
* Thick skin will provide steadfastness, and the tender heart will allow you to be transparent.
* Thick skin will prevent you from being easily offended, and the tender heart will help you learn to laugh at yourself.
* Thick skin will help you recognize the majority, but the tender heart will keep you focused on the minority.
* Thick skin will cause you to forge on through challenges, and the tender heart will keep you responsive to His presence.

No leader is perfect. There was only one perfect leader and He had an abundance of critics and even His followers doubted him from time to time. If anyone had the right to lead with thick skin and a hardened heart, it was Jesus. But He knew the right way, the better way.

Despite their greatest facades, leaders do not have all the answers. I previously mentioned one of my favorite quotes, stated at the end of Pastor Craig Groeschel's podcasts. He confidently declares, "Be yourself. People would rather follow a leader who is always real than one who is always right." Be real. Give yourself permission to feel the frustrations of leadership. Yell at God, express your disappointments, let the tears flow, and find consolation in a friend or counselor. God gave you emotions to handle every feeling connected to your faith steps.

Keep your skin thick and your heart tender. You don't have to let sin against you produce sin within you.

TEN

∎∎∎∎∎∎∎∎∎∎∎∎∎∎∎∎∎∎∎∎∎∎∎∎∎∎∎

- ASSESS -

Okay, here is the practical chapter. It's time to assess some significant areas of your life. If you're lucky, you will find yourself on the front end of drifting just in time to right the ship. For some, this chapter may reveal the ugly and unfortunate circumstances that require your immediate attention.

If you're like me, whenever you read a book with practical application questions at the end of a chapter, you skip them. Don't skip these. You need to ask yourself these questions, and you need to engage with people around you to get a 360-degree perspective. Not all of these will apply, depending on your age and stage in life, but read all of them nonetheless. If they don't apply directly to you, they may apply directly to someone else.

FAMILY

Rules of Engagement

Family is a sensitive topic. We perceive we are doing better than we are, often because our data is skewed or lacking. A wife may be fearful to speak up because of emotional or physical repercussions. A child may feel unheard or dismissed. A husband may feel berated and emasculated to the point of hopelessness. For this exercise to work, you must summon courage in order to get perspective. Proper perspective may be hard to come by, but once it is attained, it becomes the Band-Aid and the barometer. It brings healing to areas where untruth unchecked tore down your self-worth, and it enables you to gauge the atmosphere around you.

Allow me to give you a couple of rules when engaging your spouse. When wounded, our default is a defensive posture. We make inner vows refusing to be hurt by the ones closest to us and, in turn, sabotage our ability to communicate honestly without recourse. My wife and I have used these rules of engagement for years and they have served us well. I pray they are a framework for healthy conversation to come.

It's important to note, these rules are not a secret. They should be shared with each other prior to your discussion.

Rule # 1: Set a Meeting

When preparing to have a difficult conversation with your spouse, set a meeting time and place. Don't wait for the "right" time. Such a time may take weeks or months to arrive, or, worse, may have already passed. I recommend a public place. Take him/her to their favorite restaurant or a nicer restaurant than normal. For some, a public versus private setting may be irrelevant, but for most, a public setting will prevent embarrassing outbursts or painful remarks and reactions.

You may be the type to rehearse every question, response, and reaction. It won't work in this scenario, and even if you guessed right, it would not be to your advantage. You'll see why in a moment. The most important part is to plan this moment.

Rule #2: No Touching

No touching during the conversation or intimacy after. Men can have a one-track mind, and if entertaining this discussion over a nice dinner will get them a physical reward after, they may not participate at the depth needed for relational growth. If a foundation of communication has not existed prior to this meeting, you'll simply have to fight through the tension and discomfort.

Let's face it, nobody wants to be touched when the person they love and to whom they are most vulnerable enlightens them to their shortcomings. Despite your best intentions, the action may be perceived as condescending. It may also cause your significant other to feel the issue isn't as serious as you are proposing. I'm not saying you never touch, but I am recommending you avoid it during this exercise.

Rule #3: No Response

This is the toughest rule of them all. You ask the question and then say nothing. That's right, nothing. Your significant other needs to feel they can speak honestly without being interrupted, silenced, dismissed, or steamrolled. When can you respond to their answer? In twenty-four hours. You need time to separate the emotions of the moment from what's being communicated. You may be tempted to ask clarifying questions. Don't. You can ask all the questions you want in twenty-four hours. Your feedback is not the purpose of the meeting. Their perception of the circumstance is what matters. As you know, perception is reality.

Rule #4: The Return

After your significant other has answered your questions, it's your turn. I can't caution you enough—reply, don't retaliate. If you feel bruised because of their response or hurt because of their honesty, you may feel the need to punish them just the same. In doing so, you will sabotage everything you are trying to accomplish. Their comments may have come from a wounded place, but yours would come from a prideful place.

This will take a great deal of self-restraint and discipline. You or your spouse may not get it right the first couple of times. There may be too many sensitive areas for one meeting to handle. You may have to schedule one of these meetings each month for the next six months, but I promise they will get easier. The first time my wife and I went out to a nice dinner for one of these discussions, neither one of us had anything significant to discuss regarding the other person. It was nothing but positive. What at night! If this seems a like a fantasy, don't worry. You'll get there.

Now, for the questions. By no means is this a comprehensive list, but it will help you get started. Start by asking all the questions. As you repeat this practice, you'll discover some questions are more applicable than others. Keep in mind, these rules are crafted for a couple, but can easily be applied to a mentor/coaching relationship with a few subtle tweaks.

Questions to Ask Yourself:

- When was the last time I played a game with my child that they wanted to play? Was I bored or disengaged? Why?
- When was the last time I expressed genuine interest in the things my child is interested in, even if it seems silly or foolish?
- When was the last time I scheduled one-on-one time with each of my family members?
- Do I know my spouse's/significant other's/children's dreams? What do I do to show support?
- If someone only looked at my schedule and my spending, would they think my family is a priority?
- How many hours of quality time do I spend on average with my family?
- Does my job get the best of what I have to offer? Am I giving my family leftovers?
- When my spouse wants to do an activity that excites them, do I mope? Do I try to get out of it or re-schedule? Pretend to forget about it?
- Do I find other women/men more engaging than my spouse? Why?
- Do I know my family's love languages? How do I intentionally fill their love tank? (see *The 5 Love Languages* by Gary Chapman).
- Do I pray daily with my spouse? Children? (Meals don't count.)
- Have my kids ever seen me worship God? Read my Bible? Pray? Do they see it regularly? If someone asked my kids about this, what would they say?

Questions to Ask Others:

- How am I doing as a husband/wife? Where am I succeeding or struggling?
- How am I doing as a dad/mom? Where am I succeeding or struggling?
- What do I speak more frequently, life or death?
- Am I dismissive of your dreams or aspirations?
- Does my tone and body language frustrate you?
- Do you feel valued, loved, and respected by me?
- Besides God, do I make you feel you're the most important thing in my life?
- Have I wounded you with my sarcasm?
- Is there anything I've done that you've had a hard time forgiving?
- What is one behavior you'd like to see changed?
- Am I leading my home spiritually?
- (Spouse) Do you feel I'm taking you for granted?

FINANCES

- Am I tithing regularly?
- Have I allocated funds for retirement?
- Am I teaching my children how to manage money?
- How much non-mortgage debt do I have? Does my spouse know?
- Have I hidden credit cards or bills from my significant other?
- Have I established a budget with my significant other?
- How often do I have fights about money?

- On a scale of 1-10, how much financial stress is my family under? What have I done to alleviate this stress?
- Have I ever considered Financial Peace by Dave Ramsey?
- Do I support missionaries or other avenues of advancing the gospel, aside from my tithe?
- Do I find myself making impulse purchases regularly? Why?
- Do I have an emotional stronghold connected to spending?

FAITH

- Do I have a regular quiet time with God?
- Do I read my Bible daily?
- Do I attend church regularly?
- Have I discovered my spiritual gifts and made an effort to develop them?
- Can I identify the voice/promptings of Holy Spirit?
- If I talked to those around me, would they say I am spiritually mature?
- Is there a besetting sin I'm currently struggling to overcome? Who knows? How are they helping me?
- Is my attitude toward God one of blame or gratitude?
- Who am I having a hard time forgiving? What would it take to release that person from their mistake or offense?
- Am I divisive? (Ask this of a leader in authority.)
- Has anyone ever said I am prideful?
- Who am I pointing toward Jesus? Discipling? Do people outside of church know I am a Christian? Why or why not?

PURPOSE

- Have I identified my purpose?
- How am I fulfilling my purpose?
- Who have I compared myself to recently? Did it make me feel superior or inferior? (Either way, I lose.)
- Have I allowed someone else's opinion of me to cause me to drift?
- Who in my life can I be completely honest with, no matter the question?
- Do I have a plan to fulfill my purpose? Who knows my plan?
- When is the last time I allowed someone to hold me accountable to my purpose?
- Is my purpose God driven or self-driven?
- What has distracted me from my purpose?
- Do I allow my significant other to speak into my purpose?
- Have I aligned myself with others who have a similar purpose?
- Have I given up on my purpose? If so, why? And who can I share this with to find encouragement and direction.

ELEVEN

. . . .

FORTIFY

Fortifying your decision to stay on course and fight against the drift is essential, but your fortification is not as simple as keeping external influences out. It's also about keeping the right stuff within. You will exhaust yourself as you use every tool at your disposal to fend off the urges, destructive patterns, and degrading behaviors. And the moment you make any sort of mistake, you will be tempted to throw all your efforts away and fall headfirst into the drift.

That being said, self-control still matters, but not in the way you would think. Within all of us is a desire to control our destiny, and whether you realize it or not, this desire often finds its origin in fear, not kingdom intention. Fear leads to insecurity, insecurity leads to control, control leads to manipulation, and manipulation leads to division, ruined relationships, and distrust.

I get it. You simply want to do your part in creating a healthy environment; however, when Holy Spirit is left out of the conversation and Jesus' act of grace on the cross is devalued, the result is excess control we erroneously confuse for biblical self-control. All extremes are dysfunctional, and we tip toward dysfunctional self-control when we attempt to fix everything at once, with our willpower and giving ourselves no room for error. It's perfection or nothing. Yet the spiritual healing you crave will be inept if your efforts for control become dysfunctional.

Biblical self-control is not found in willpower. It is the profound self-awareness of your own limitations and the refusal to trust in your own strength. Biblical self-control is the continual submission to the will of the Father and the passionate pursuit fully implementing the mind of Christ in every decision.

There is a lot said in the Scriptures about self-control. We know it is a fruit of the Spirit (Galatians 5:22–23) and the result of a life lived in Christ. Proverbs adds beautiful and sober imagery to self-control and allows us to view it not in theory but in practice. It creates the image of a person's life as a city. Cities are often placed near water in order to irrigate crops and provide the things needed for day-to-day activities.

The city was frequently placed in a position where it could most easily defend itself against raiding parties or enemy armies. The walls were thick, tall, and meant to protect the people within as well as keep intruders out. One city that stands out in the Old Testament is Jericho. It was a behemoth, and much like the Titanic, it appeared invincible. Let's look at this great city's dimensions.

The mound, or "tell," of Jericho was surrounded by a great earthen rampart, or embankment, with a stone retaining wall at its base. The retaining wall was some twelve to fifteen feet high. On top of that was a mudbrick wall six feet thick and about twenty to twenty-six feet high. At the crest of the embankment was a similar mudbrick wall whose base was roughly forty-six feet above the ground level outside the retaining wall. This is what loomed high above the Israelites as they marched around the city each day for seven days. Humanly speaking, it was impossible for the Israelites to penetrate the impregnable bastion of Jericho.

What does this have to do with self-control? *Everything.*

It doesn't matter how strong your desire, how great your ambition, or how mighty your resolve. If you lack self-control, you are simply inviting the enemy into the fortified city of your life. No matter how great the walls, one area where self-control is absent can cost us *everything*. Here are a few examples.

FOOD

Lack of self-control with regard to food affects energy and invites sickness and disease. The Mayo Clinic lists heart disease, type 2 diabetes, certain cancers, digestive problems, sleep apnea, sexual problems and osteoarthritis as complications stemming from overeating. This limits your ability to do what God has called you to do. It allows for excuses, embarrassment, and lack of confidence, and can lead to an early death leaving behind a family who was robbed to soon of your love, presence, and support.

"All things are lawful for me," but not all things are helpful. "All things are lawful for me," but I will not be dominated by anything" (1 Corinthians 6:12 ESV).

DRUGS/ALCOHOL

Coming from a family that has a history of alcohol abuse, I see the immediate impacts. Wasted money, lack of financial security, verbal and physical abuse, neglect, etc.

"Do not get drunk on wine, which leads to debauchery. Instead, be filled with the Spirit" (Ephesians 5:18).

"Be sober-minded; be watchful. Your adversary the devil prowls around like a roaring lion, seeking someone to devour" (1 Peter 5:8 ESV)

SEX

An addiction to sex can (outside of marriage) destroys a life, both within marriage and outside of marriage in so many ways. If married, affairs destroy trust, break apart the family unit, and ruin relationships. Other areas such as bestiality, pedophilia, homosexuality, rape, sex trafficking, and pornography all come from a refusal to submit to the kingdom perspective of sex.

"For this is the will of God, your sanctification: that you abstain from sexual immorality; that each one of you know how to control his own body in holiness and honor, not in the passion of lust like the Gentiles who do not know God" (1 Thessalonians 4:3–5 ESV).

SLEEP/LAZINESS

People who refuse to get up waste time and are ineffective. They lack control of their schedule and in doing so force others to dictate their pace instead of taking control of their own lives. Consider God's perspective of laziness:

I went past the field of a sluggard, past the vineyard of someone who has no sense; thorns had come up every-

where, the ground was covered with weeds and the stone wall was in ruins. I applied my heart to what I observed and learned a lesson from what I saw: A little sleep, a little slumber, a little folding of the hands to rest—and poverty will come on you like a thief and scarcity like an armed man. (Proverbs 24:30–34)

SET THE GUARDRAILS

In the previous chapter, you assessed multiple areas of your life. Now it's time to fortify your city, and it starts with guardrails. In his compelling series titled *Guardrails*, Andy Stanley makes a profound observation. He states:

Guardrails protect us from what lurks on the other side. The danger zone. You never see guardrails on long, flat stretches of road. They're in the sharp curves and along the sheer cliffs. Yes, they can dent your bumper and bust your headlight. But all that lies on the other side of the guardrail could do far greater damage. I have to confess I'm not a highway safety expert. But I've spent years watching people make wrecks out of their lives. And the principle of the guardrail applies on the road and in your life. Your greatest regret in life probably could have been avoided if you had protected yourself from the danger zone—if you had established some guardrails. Personal guardrails are boundaries you establish on the safe side of damaging decisions that protect you from the danger ahead. They're meant to set off warning bells over seemingly little things...little things that can lead to big, messy consequences."

The beauty of guardrails is found in the drift. They are de-signed to provide enough space to operate, but when the margin runs out, they quickly alert you to the error of your ways. Guardrails are essential for every person, not just those who have frequently fallen short. As Andy Stanley so accurately explains, guardrails are intentionally positioned in safe places to prevent you from being in-jured or destroyed.

Guardrails aren't some set of rules that magically keep you safe. Done right, they are built off convictions that lead to principles. Those principles become the gatekeepers of your thoughts and ac-tions. Every decision you make must filter through those principles. If decision does not align with your principles, it must be swiftly termi-nated. No thought or decision can be allowed to linger. As I stated in chapter 1, the believer who can lead their thoughts is capable of achieving the impossible.

Allow me to provide a few personal examples, knowing these may look different for everyone. First, I'll give the principle, then I'll give the guardrails that enable me to live by that principle, then I'll spell out the implications.

PRINCIPLE #1: Next to God, my wife is the most important person in my life.

Guardrail 1: I do not allow myself to be alone with a member of the opposite sex.

* I do not allow a member of the opposite sex to ride in my car without someone else present.
* I do not go out to eat, get coffee, or participate in activities alone with someone of the opposite sex.

Guardrail 2: My wife has access to my phone and all email and social media accounts.

* My wife has freedom to check my phone at any moment, including my text messages and browser history.
* My wife and I both use location apps (currently Life360), so she not only knows where I am at any given moment, but also where I've been. This isn't about control. It's about giving her every reason to trust me.

Guardrail 3: Physical distance matters.

* I should limit the physical interaction, including long hugs, frontal hugs, and other manners of physical affection or acknowledgement, with the opposite sex.
* I will not flirt, even in jest, with members of the opposite sex.

Guardrail 4: I will protect my wife's integrity.

* I will not speak badly of my wife to friends or family.
* I will defend my wife from accusation.
* I will place her in situations where she is looked upon favorably.

PRINCIPLE #2: I will be a good steward of what God has given me.

  Guardrail 1: I give God the **first** 10 percent of my income.

* I set up auto-pay, so my tithe is automatically deducted from my pay.
* I set up my bill pay schedule to ensure I'm not overstretched and tempted to use my tithe for other things.

Guardrail 2: I will not spend over $100 without first discussing it with my wife.

* I do not have credit cards she's unaware of.
* I do not hide bank statements.
* We hold budget meetings to review spending.
* We share a budgeting app (currently EveryDollar Plus) so she can see spending in real time.

Guardrail 3: I will leave an inheritance for my children and grandchildren.

* I invest regularly to retirement.
* I set aside money for children's education.
* I have created a will/trust.

PRINCIPLE #3: I will guard my ear gates and eye gates.

Guardrail 1: I will play only appropriate music.

* I do not play anything with profanity.
* I play more worship/Christian music than anything else.

Guardrail 2: I will establish filters.

* On all devices.
* On streaming services.
* On the computer.
* Covenant Eyes / Netsanity are great accountability options

Guardrail 3: No movies or shows rated MA.

* I set a restriction on devices and streaming services.
* I have a spouse or friend set the PIN code.

You must choose to live by emotions or live by principles. Principles and guardrails work hand in hand to protect you when your self-control falters and allow you to live a regret-free life.

YOUR ANONYMOUS YEARS

The road back may seem overwhelming. When all you've known is drifting, living with intention becomes a daunting task; however, this is exactly why we learn to acknowledge our weaknesses and present them to the Lord daily. J. Hudson Taylor, a well-known British missionary to China, said it this way: "I have found that there are three stages in every great work of God: first, it is impossible, then it is difficult, then it is done."

Right now it may seem impossible. Perhaps you should disregard the notion of perfection for a season. Perhaps you should simply strive for "difficult." Then, after some time, you may find the work of God completed and perfected in you.

You must spend a disproportionate amount of time, shifting from thin and shallow to deep and wide. Many of us have heard about the infamous iceberg illustration—90 percent hidden, 10 percent revealed. We marvel at the 10 percent long before we ever see the 90 percent.

In her book *Anonymous*, Alicia Britt Chole addressed Jesus' hidden years, the 90 percent He lived in obscurity. She remarks that it is not the 10 percent, but the 90 percent that makes the iceberg indestructible. It's not the 10 percent visibility of Jesus but the 90 percent obscurity that made Him indestructible.

She states, "However, when we state our desire to 'be like Jesus,' we are not referring to Jesus' anonymous years. 'I want to walk like Jesus walked and live like Jesus lived!' is generally not equated in our hearts with, 'I want to live 90 percent of my life in absolute obscurity!'" How many of us would say that we want to live 90 percent of our lives being hidden? There are innate passions that desire to propel us toward achieving, succeeding, and being known.

We want our greatest gifts, talents, and abilities to be revealed to all. We *want* to be known. We *want* to be seen. We *want* to be praised. Jesus wanted to be hidden.

Revelation before formation is a weight few can carry. If Jesus refused to be seen before His formation was complete, who are we to expect different? Why are the hidden times of life painted in a negative light? Shouldn't we long for the hiddenness? Is that what Jesus meant when He said, "Blessed are the meek, for they will inherit the earth" (Matthew 5:5)?

Maybe I'll create my own beatitude. Blessed are those who are hidden, for the formation they experience during obscurity will be what sustains them when they are made known.

Chole adds, "In other words, trials tell us less about our future than they do about our past. Why? Because the decisions we make in difficult places today are greatly the product of decisions we made in unseen places of our yesterdays."

This is your time to fortify. This is your time to build strength and depth and confidence. This is your time to establish principles, and guardrails help keep you focused on the future impact you'll make for the kingdom of God. You've moved past the past. Now it's time to ensure the walls don't fall when the first attack comes.

PAYING IT FORWARD

It's popular in both religious and non-religious circles. You'll find the phrase frequently used in men's groups and in pop-culture magazines. It's been used as the title of multiple cinematic and literary works, and even if you've never cracked open a Bible, you likely know that the term *brother's keeper* originated within its pages.

God asked a masterful question to Cain: "Where is your brother, Abel?" It may not seem like a profound question on the surface, but it elicited the self-condemning response He was after. Cain suspected he'd skirt the question with another question, hoping God would just move on, but all it did was further show how disconnected his relationship was with his creator. In that moment, he wrongly assumed God's feedback loop was limited.

Of course, God knew Abel's location, and Cain's response proved that he knew his brother's location as well. "I do not know. Am I my brother's keeper?" It was a pain-filled response. It was a response of regret, and his language exposed his shame.

In the Old Testament, "to keep" means to watch over, to guard. The role of a "keeper" is the role of a bodyguard. A protector. An overwatch. Cain's use of the word was not in context with the question. Cain gave the worst response possible. He could have said, "I last saw him on the hillside," or "He was tending to the sheep." Both of those would have been lies, but they would not have been self-condemning.

In using the word *keeper*, Cain showed he was aware of harm that had happened to Abel. "Am I his bodyguard? Am I responsible for keeping him from harm? Am I supposed to watch over him every second of every day to ensure he doesn't get hurt?"

159

In saying he "did not know" Abel's location, he unknowingly admitted he was the offender. God asked for a location, and Cain gave Him a confession. How do we know it was a confession? Because of God's follow-up question: "What have you done?"

God does not question us for His understanding, but for ours. He leads us to search out our inner demons and expose them so that we may be free. He uncovers our motives and presents us with an opportunity to deal with them.

Cain's response condemned him but empowers us. God never directly answered Cain's question. He did not say, "Yes, Cain, you are your brother's keeper," but He made his intention clear through Cain's harsh punishment. To answer the question, yes, you are your brother's (or sister's) keeper. You are to be their overwatch, to guard them, to protect them.

In a self-serving world, it is not uncommon for people to use their brother or sister as a steppingstone to their own advancement. It's not uncommon in the business world, or even the church world, to throw them under the proverbial bus. It may make them look better, wiser, or more loyal, but what they leave behind is a pain-soaked trail, littered with relational roadkill.

There are times when the assault on our brother or sister is intentional. There are times when it is done out of ignorance. Discerning leaders know the difference. They have an uncanny ability to see through the noise. When all one brings is bad news about their brother or sister, chances are, you're dealing with a Cain spirit. If they exalt themselves by disparaging others, you might be dealing with a Cain spirit. If they downplay their successes and promote their shortcomings, you might be dealing with a Cain spirit.

Unfortunately, gossip is often rewarded with proximity. There is nothing to be personally gained by shielding your brother's or sister's shortcomings and proclaiming their successes. Nothing of this earth, anyway. But it certainly matters to God.

"Let each of you look not only to his own interests, but also to the interests of others" (Philippians 2:4 ESV).

"Above all, keep loving one another earnestly, since love covers a multitude of sins" (1 Peter 4:8 ESV).

"But love your enemies, and do good, and lend, expecting nothing in return, and your reward will be great, and you will be sons of the Most High, for he is kind to the ungrateful and evil" (Luke 6:35 ESV)

"Bear one another's burdens, and so fulfill the law of Christ" (Galatians 6:2 ESV).

God is a rewarder. He rewarded Abel when he brought the proper sacrifice. He rewards those who ultimately "keep" their brother or sister as well. Yes, it *is* your responsibility to guard your brother and sister. After all, it's much better to align yourself with Abel and give your life, than to align yourself with Cain and take a life that doesn't belong to you.

Thankfully, Jesus felt the same way when He gave his life instead of taking ours. *"Greater love has no one than this, that someone lay down his life for his friends" (John 15:13 ESV).*

TWELVE

ATTACK

THE WARRIOR AND THE CHILD

One of my favorite songs when I was a youth pastor was "The Warrior Is a Child" by Twila Paris. I would play it on the piano during my treasured quiet time with God. I remember it like it was yesterday, as I walked into the dark sanctuary lit only by the stage lights. I would spend hours there on my face in prayer. It was a special place of peace. As much as I fought for what was right, there were moments when juvenile mistakes, sin, and self-doubt left me disarmed in His presence. I couldn't fight when all I could think about was how I had drifted.

The warrior and the child both exist in the life of the believer. There are moments when you'll storm hell with a squirt gun, and then there are moments when the mere threat of another person will send you on a suicidal pilgrimage (1 Kings 19).

I guess in light of our relationship with God, we cannot always be the warrior. After all, it wasn't the faith of a warrior that Jesus asked for. The child within needs space to breathe, find comfort in the Father, and train in the Spirit so the warrior can succeed in the battle. The child needs to know they can run to God when they fall. The child-like heart is why we are willing to sprint to God regardless of what we're wearing, where we've been, what we've seen, what we've spoken, or who we've become.

Being a father has enlightened me to how God sees us. If you are a parent, you've likely had the same aha moments. The other day my daughter was jumping on the couch while I was doing dishes. She was all hopped up on ice cream, and while we don't let her jump on the couch, she took advantage of my busyness to do so.

Suddenly, a loud sound echoed through our home. She had tripped over the pillow and fell face first onto the flat armrest of the sofa. Her tears flowed immediately, and every worst-case scenario flashed before my mind in a split second. Had she broken her nose? Did she land on her teeth, pushing them back? I ran over and saw blood coming from her mouth.

All she wanted in that moment was Daddy. She gripped my neck tight and for a minute wouldn't let go. I wanted to immediately assess the damage, but all she wanted was to hold her daddy and hear me tell her everything was going to be okay. After a couple of minutes, we sat in the bathroom and I was able to take a look.

The blood came from just a little cut on the inside of her top lip, but to her it was the worst thing that ever happened to her. She was scared and didn't know what to do. I just kept telling her, "It's okay. It's not bad. You're going to be all right." A few minutes later she was sitting on the couch, eating a popsicle to help the swelling go down. She was ready to start jumping again.

There are times in our lives when God's perspective of our pain is not the same as ours. In our most troubled moments, the world seems to be crashing all around us and we are scared, hurt, and don't know what to do. Father God looks at our wounds and whispers, "It's okay. It's not that bad. You're going to be all right." We may not believe him, but he's right. What made me proud was my daughter's willingness to believe her daddy and her resilience to get back onto the proverbial horse (even though we don't want her to).

We relate to people most often from our warrior side. It's not that we want to, it's just a natural reaction from life's experiences. However, we pray against that because it's more important that our armor is God's armor, not ours. It's easy to cling to the warrior within, viewing the child as weak and ineffective. Yet in God's upside-down kingdom, the faith of a child is the prerequisite to conquering nations.

The irony is that the warrior and the child must coexist. One without the other accomplishes little. They balance each other. Too much child and nothing gets conquered, although great intentions exist. Too much warrior and the fighting overcomes obedience, and we conquer but don't think about the ramifications. The child keeps the warrior focused on what's right, and the warrior keeps the child from shrinking toward inactivity. Sometimes we must drop our swords and allow God to minister to the child within, so the warrior can win more battles.

THE PRAYING WARRIOR. THE PRAYING CHILD.

One of the sweetest things I'd ever heard was my daughter praying. She blessed Meemaw, Pap Pap, Mimi, Jackie, Mommy, Daddy, and Uncle Tommy. She also blessed the curtains and the wall and the crib, but maybe those needed it too. It was so sincere. Even though she could not grasp the power or meaning of the word *intercession*, I believe she was engaging her inner spiritual warrior and talking to her Father on behalf of the people she loved.

Charles Spurgeon once said, "If you believe in prayer at all, expect God to hear you. If you do not expect, you will not have. God will not hear you unless you believe He will hear you; but if you believe He will, He will be as good as your faith." My daughter believes every prayer she prays is heard by God and answered by God. She has the faith of a child, and the faith of a child enveloped with the persistence, patience, and power of a warrior will accomplish impossible feats.

To fight against the drift, intercession must be the sharpest tool in your arsenal. Prayer is not about checking off a list of needs. It's about taking back what Adam had given away in the garden of Eden. It's about authority, and warriors know about authority. Martin Luther King Jr. declared, "To be a Christian without prayer is no more possible than to be alive without breathing."

Prayer is an offensive weapon, but we are better known for using it defensively. When I read Ephesians 6, I'm encouraged to unleash my inner warrior. Just read this.

Finally, be strong in the Lord and in his mighty power. Put on the full armor of God, so that you can take your stand against the devil's schemes. For our struggle is not against flesh and blood, but against the rulers, against the authorities, against the powers of this dark world and against the spiritual forces of evil in the heavenly realms. Therefore put on the full armor of God, so that when the day of evil comes, you may be able to stand your ground, and after you have done everything, to stand. Stand firm then, with the belt of truth buckled around your waist, with the breastplate of righteousness in place, and with your feet fitted with the readiness that comes from the gospel of peace. In addition to all this, take up the shield of faith, with which you can extinguish all the flaming arrows of the evil one. Take the helmet of salvation and the sword of the Spirit, which is the word of God. And pray in the Spirit on all occasions with all kinds of prayers and requests. With this in mind, be alert and always keep on praying for all the Lord's people. (Ephesians 6:10–18)

The apostle Paul is the spiritual version of two of my favorite movies, *Braveheart* and *Gladiator*. The armor pieces discussed in verses 11–17 are so valuable. This passage reveals the mandatory battle-ready uniform for spiritual warfare. It prepares the warrior to fight. But it's what happens in verse 18 that brings perfect clarity. If we refuse to pray in the Spirit, we will end up fighting the wrong battles and our armor will be damaged by confrontations that were never supposed to happen. Through prayer we find our battle plan, in His presence the child becomes a warrior, and through intercession we unleash the power of God working in and through us to change the world.

Isaiah 52:12 says, "But you will not leave in haste or go in flight; for the Lord will go before you, the God of Israel will be your rear guard." When you are overcoming the drift, don't turn back! Don't retreat! As a child of God, retreat is no longer in your arsenal, not because of your strength but because of the all-powerful God we serve. Don't even look back, because our ever-present God is not just before you, he's behind you. He's protecting your back from an enemy who will not play by your rules. He's got you.

Keep. Moving. Forward.

"For though we walk in the flesh, we are not waging war according to the flesh. For the weapons of our warfare are not of the flesh but have divine power to destroy strongholds" (2 Corinthians 10:4 ESV).

LOVE IS A WEAPON

When reading the story of Moses and the exodus, I can't help but think about the prayers. The prayers for deliverance. The prayers for justice. The prayers for freedom. The prayers for peace. The prayers for rest. The prayers for mercy. Some of the Israelites had never known these words in action. They'd only known captivity, and they were convinced that captivity was normal. How do you convince someone of their need for something more, when they feel like they are getting exactly what they deserve?

You may be familiar with these prayers. You may have prayed them before. You may be praying them right now. Or you may be so immersed in hopelessness that you've stopped praying them completely. After all, if God heard and He cared, why has He not answered them?

This is the problem, isn't it? We see Scripture after Scripture, promise after promise to answer, yet we feel shunned. We feel neglected. We may even feel jealous as He pours out blessing after blessing on others.

I'm frustrated by this story and I'm moved emotionally by this story. "I have indeed seen the misery of my people in Egypt. ... I have heard them crying out ... and I am concerned about their suffering."

In moments of darkness, I'd like to believe God has overlooked my plight, but I'd be wrong. God sees. God hears. God is concerned. God moves on our behalf. I'm not sure we will ever understand the simple complexity of God's love. We can turn away from others and proclaim, "Because of what they've done, I don't love them." We can shout with conviction that, "I have fallen out of love with him/her." But the reality is **God can't.**

Our mistakes will never be enough for Father God to not love us. Our rejection will not make Him love us less. We can curse Him, hate Him, and turn our backs on Him, but His love is unconditional. It's still there. I can't imagine how hard that would be emotionally—to be abused, spit on, and rejected, yet not be able to tame the unconditional love and passion for humanity.

I think what I hate about this story is that freedom didn't help. God delivered His people physically, but mentally they never let go of Egypt. They never learned the love of the Father. They constantly doubted His character, His provision, and His faithfulness, and in turn they searched for, fashioned, and praised the cheapest of substitutes.

This is the harsh negative of limited love. Love is within our control, but we choose not to lead in it. Limited love is reactionary. Is this why we get angry when God doesn't do as we think He should? Is it because our perspective of love could be wistfully inadequate? Is it because we think in error that somehow God could fall out of love with us? Is that why He hasn't answered? Does my misery move Him? Does He even care?

Yes. He does. He has to. He has seen your misery, He has heard your cries, and He is moved with compassion and concern for your suffering. Hold on a little longer. Wait for Him. His love is unfailing. His love causes Him to fight for you. His love causes Him to defend you. His love calls Him into battle, and His power prepares a place at the victor's table. Never underestimate the power of love as a weapon. Never underestimate, in your circumstance, how love can heal. Look at these examples found in Scripture:

"Let the morning bring me word of your unfailing love, for I have put my trust in you. Show me the way I should go, for to you I entrust my life" (Psalm 143:8).

"In your unfailing love you will lead the people you have redeemed" (Exodus 15:13).

"Turn, Lord, and deliver me; save me because of your unfailing love" (Psalm 6:4).

"But I trust in your unfailing love; my heart rejoices in your salvation" (Psalm 13:5).

"When I said, 'My foot is slipping,' your unfailing love, Lord, supported me" (Psalm 94:18).

"For everyone who has been born of God overcomes the world. And this is the victory that has overcome the world—our faith" (1 John 5:4 ESV).

If you are feeling hopeless right now, please hear me. If you call, He *will* answer. He'll come to your rescue. Unfailing love beckons Him to us in an unavoidable way, and His love is always associated with action. He loves, so He redeems. He loves, so He delivers. He loves, so He saves. He loves, so He supports.

He loves *you*, His warrior, His child.

CONCLUSION

So Joshua called together the twelve men he had appointed from the Israelites, one from each tribe, and said to them, "Go over before the ark of the Lord your God into the middle of the Jordan. Each of you is to take up a stone on his shoulder, according to the number of the tribes of the Israelites, to serve as a sign among you. In the future, when your children ask you, 'What do these stones mean?' tell them that the flow of the Jordan was cut off before the ark of the covenant of the Lord. When it crossed the Jordan, the waters of the Jordan were cut off. These stones are to be a memorial to the people of Israel forever." (Joshua 4:4–7)

What altar will you establish to signify your life change? What will you tell the generations to come? How will you explain the moment you stopped drifting and started living with intentionality? Your story is still being written, but there is no better time to build an altar than now.

There are moments during this walk with Christ when we experience victory, power, and presence in a way that is truly life changing. It's as if the cosmos comes to a halt as the divine interrupts the daily routine just for you and for me. What was natural and expected bows before the supernatural and unexpected as God once again pours out His love upon our circumstances to "make things all right" again. When we read Scripture, those moments are so moving and powerful that humanity can't help but build an altar, a place of remembrance.

I suppose it's fitting. There is something to be said, and something to be told, about that moment in our history. The moment when God heard our cries, God saw our tears, and our prayers echoed through the heavens so loudly that He could not hold back His power any longer.

Unleashing a small measure of His omnipotence, He moved under the unconquerable mission of love to come to our rescue. More often than not do we deserve such an encounter, but receive it we must. We do not always deserve such an encounter, but He desires us to receive it, nonetheless.

It is, was, and always will be for our benefit.

So, it's fitting to build an altar. A place of remembrance. A place that is forever anchored in our conscience and spirit. A place where we draw strength, comfort, assurance, confidence, and restoration.

Two very specific songs come to my mind during times of stress, fatigue, frustration, and loneliness. Both are older songs— songs that may have been forgotten or, for some, have yet to be heard. For me, they are established altars of remembrance. When I hear them, I can't help but travel through time to the moment He met me at my worst and gave me His best. I did not write them, but they are mine. You likely have your own songs, images, poems, or books that mark moments of God's faithfulness. Don't ever let them go. They are *your* altars of remembrance.

Altars are scriptural and they are often necessary. While we can never change the past, we can often draw encouragement from past experiences. One day our children may ask what those altars are for. They may ask why we are emotionally moved when a twenty-year-old song begins to play. They may ask why we cherish certain people or places.

They'll ask and you'll be blessed to tell them, "That, my child, is when God showed up and changed my life. **I had drifted, but He brought me back."**

Following Jesus

If you have drifted away from Jesus, it's time to come home. He loves you and gave His life for you. If you're ready to repent of your sins and ask God for forgiveness, repeat after me.

"Jesus, I believe in you. I believe you are the son of God who died for my sins and rose again. I confess that I'm a sinner and I ask you to forgive me. Today, I commit my life to following you. Amen."

If you said that prayer, **CONGRATULATIONS**! I would love to hear from you. If you accepted Christ after reading this book please visit my website, www.twtwigg.com, and send me a message. You are about to begin the greatest journey of your life. Keep moving forward.

NOTES

Chapter 1:
Inception (2010), *IMDb*, https://www.imdb.com/title/tt1375666/.

"Sydney J. Harris > Quotes > Quotable Quote," *Goodreads*, https://www.goodreads.com/quotes/27458-when-i-hear-somebody-sigh-life-is-hard-i-am.

Dr. Deborah Waterbury, *The Lies that Bind: And the Truth that Sets Us Free* (DebWaterbury, Inc., 2017, xvi.

Rich Morin, "The Difficult Transition from Military to Civilian Life," *Pew Research Center*, December 8, 2011, https://www.pewsocialtrends.org/2011/12/08/the-difficult-transition-from-military-to-civilian-life/.

Robert L. Thomas, *New American Standard Hebrew-Aramaic and Greek Dictionaries : Updated Edition* (Anaheim: Foundation Publications, Inc., 1998).

Chapter 2:
"William Carey Quotes," *Brainy Quote*, https://www.brainyquote.com/quotes/william_carey_191985.

John Piper, *When the Darkness Will Not Lift: Doing What We Can While We Wait for God—and Joy* (Wheaton, IL: Crossway Books, 2006), 16.

"Henry Ford Quotes," *Brainy Quote*, https://www.brainyquote.com/quotes/henry_ford_121339.\

Chapter 3:

"Craig Groeschel Leadership Podcast: It's About Time, Part 2," *Open Network*, https://open.life.church/training/109-leadership-podcast-it-s-about-time-part-2.

https://www.aol.com/article/news/2017/05/19/millennials-expected-to-take-over-25-000-selfies-in-their-lifeti/22099995/

Jamie Ducharme, "More Millennials Are Dying 'Deaths of Despair," as Overdose and Suicide Rates Climb," *Time*, June 13, 2019, https://time.com/5606411/millennials-deaths-of-despair/.

Jamie Ducharme, "Young Americans Are the Loneliest, According to a New Study," *Time*, May 1, 2018, https://time.com/5261181/young-americans-are-lonely/.

Bob Goff's Facebook page, posted December 30, 2018, https://www.facebook.com/bobgoffis/posts/god-never-compares-what-he-creates/2359312907477302/.

Chapter 4:

Stephen M. R. Covey, *The SPEED of TRUST: The One Thing That Changes Everything* (New York: Free Press, 2018), 13.

Chapter 5:

Mike Connaway, *Sabotage: The Nasty Little Secret We All Know Holds Us Back!* (Tulsa, OK: Insight Publishing Group, 2003).

Rick Warren, *The Purpose Driven Life: What on Earth Am I Here For?* (Grand Rapids, MI: Zondervan, 2012), 248___.

Chapter 7:

Brennan Manning, *The Signature of Jesus* (Colorado Springs, CO: Multnomah Books, 1996), 14.

Haddon Robinson, *What Jesus Said about Successful Living: Principles from the Sermon on the Mount* (Grand Rapids, MI: Discovery House Publishers, 1991), eBook.

J. A. Redhead, *Finding Meaning in the Beatitudes* (Nashville: Abingdon Press, 1968), 37.

Chapter 11:

"The Walls of Jericho," *Bible Study Tools*, https://www.biblestudytools.com/blogs/associates-for-biblical-research/the-walls-of-jericho.html.

https://www.mayoclinic.org/diseases-conditions/obesity/symptoms-causes/syc-20375742

Andy Stanley, "Guardrails: Avoiding Regrets in Your Life," *Sermon Central*, September 6, 2011, https://www.sermoncentral.com/pastors-preaching-articles/andy-stanley-guardrails-avoiding-regrets-in-your-life-1028.

"James Hudson Taylor > Quotes > Quotable Quote," *Goodreads*, https://www.goodreads.com/quotes/335717-there-are-three-stages-to-every-great-work-of-god.

Alicia Britt Chole, *Anonymous* (Nashville: Thomas Nelson, 2006), 9-10.

Ibid, 15..

Chapter 12:

"Martin Luther King Jr. > Quotes > Quotable Quote," *Goodreads*, https://www.goodreads.com/quotes/602419-to-be-a-christian-without-prayer-is-no-more-possible.

Books by Bob Rhoden

 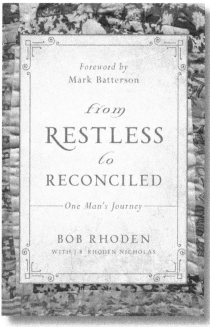

Develop Your Leadership.
Make a Difference.

CPSIA information can be obtained
at www.ICGtesting.com
Printed in the USA
BVHW030221070421
604350BV00029B/105/J